THE
UNDISCOVERED
COUNTRY

ANDRE BAGOO

THE
UNDISCOVERED
COUNTRY

ESSAYS

PEEPAL TREE

First published in Great Britain in 2020
Peepal Tree Press Ltd
17 King's Avenue
Leeds LS6 1QS
England

ISBN13: 97818452324638

Supported using public funding by
ARTS COUNCIL
ENGLAND

CONTENTS

The world is an idea.

– Arthur Schopenhauer

INTRODUCTION

In answer to a complex question, Baudelaire has a simple answer. What is art? he asks. His response? Prostitution. This might seem a provocation until we appreciate how both involve the human body, the exchange of money, the mobilisation of market forces, the gaze of an onlooker, the commissioning of illicit acts, the subversion of ordinary relations, the showing up of forms of power, the disavowal of authority, the rejection of absolutes, the expression of needs, the satisfaction of wants. At least for Baudelaire art was in good company; he linked prostitution to love.

This book of essays is concerned with art and politics. Art, whether prostitution or not, is the necessary precursor to politics.

Art encourages us to look, to reflect, and, in the process, to re-imagine. It provokes opinions. It encourages people to speak up, to add their voices to a discourse that, over time, flows like a river, eroding the banks of ignorance. It transports and spreads ideas, sorting and refining the sediment of controversy, nourishing the floodplain of society.

Art is the diversity of the body politic made manifest. It is the granting of visibility to the hitherto invisible. Art shows us people and perspectives we might never otherwise encounter or understand. As Habermas argues, democracy cannot thrive if citizens cannot speak.

Politics is an art. At times it is built on honest ideas, at other times deceptions. Always, it is about style and the exercise of power. It is a fictional narrative, the arc of history, a long epic written and re-written by bards of varying skill.

These essays have been written in the spirit of such ideas. They do not set out merely to report. They castigate and praise. They aim to provoke, to add fuel to the fire of argumentation, the ceaseless discourse on the shape of a place. They make public the private through the trick vessel of art.

In 15th century Europe, "to essay" was to test the quality of something. The Old French word *essai* meant trial. A critic of literature or the visual arts is a political animal, someone with a point of view who, implicitly or not, argues for a version of the world.

Little wonder the essay has certain attractions for poets. "Both poetry and the essay come from the same impulse," Marianne Boruch says, "to think about something and at the same time, see it closely, carefully, and enact it."

The essay, like the poem, has a variety of costumes. It is deeply forgiving: capable of accommodating the polemical, the comic, the visual, the poetic. The Chinese, after the fall of the Han dynasty, created essays that alloyed prose and verse. In this vein, ideas about society flow naturally from the belief that art, art criticism and politics go hand in hand. I am just as interested in observing the world as reading the text – particularly when the one throws light on the other. This book discusses food, film, music and other forms of culture that infuse literature. Though Trinidad looms large, another republic is in view.

While some speak of the rebirth of the essay, the truth is that it has never been out of style. Even today, when people say print is passé, the novel dead, poetry irrelevant, and theatre arcane, essays come to us in an unending stream of newspaper columns, social media posts, diatribes by trolls, comments on online forums, blogs, vlogs, podcasts and websites dedicated to ideas.

Perhaps the essay has never been out of style because it has always been about one thing: its writer. Essays on literature, art, material culture and on politics can be a form of self-care, an affirmation of the value of all perspectives whether we agree or not. When she wrote about Kafka, Margaret Atwood acknowledged that "My real subject was not the author of the books but the author of the essay, me." Here, then, is a history of myself told in many voices, ranging across genres and nations. Here, to repurpose a Shakespearean phrase, is the undiscovered country.

THE LAST PAGE

Some say time has run its course and that the life we lead is no more than the fading reflection of an event beyond recall. W.G. Sebald observed that we simply do not know how many of its possible mutations the world may have already gone through, or how much time, assuming that it exists, remains.

I like to think about this when I consider V.S. Naipaul and Derek Walcott. Imagine a reality in which neither man became world-famous, in which both stayed in the Caribbean, never leaving to write, travel or live elsewhere. See them holding down office jobs, Walcott plodding along as an arts reporter for a newspaper, Naipaul working as a copy writer, or maybe even a civil servant in the Red House. In this world, neither becomes a Nobel laureate for literature. Nor do they end up mortal enemies. Walcott does not write that poem comparing Naipaul to a mongoose. Naipaul does not write that essay dismissing Walcott as being lost in an imitative swamp. In this world, they meet and become good friends. Their shared passion is writing: a hobby they view from afar. They spend their days in the drudgery of office work, and spend their nights drinking, smoking, talking about Nietzsche, Sartre, Heidegger or whichever philosopher is fashionable at the time.

Whenever I read *Miguel Street*, this fantasy of mine comes to mind. There is a specific moment in Naipaul's book, a brief, slight moment, a mere sliver of time, in which a character says something so profound it could well be the key to unravelling all these different worlds.

"Look, boys, it ever strike you that the world not real at all?" the self-taught teacher Titus Hoyte says. "It ever strike you that we have the only mind in the world and you just thinking up everything else? Like me here, having the only mind in the world, and thinking up you people here, thinking up the war and all the houses and the ships and them in the harbour. That ever cross your mind?"

In Naipaul's hands we are meant to laugh at Hoyte. The fact that he is self-made is not admirable. Rather, it is a kind of hubris, meant to underline his status as an outsider, a person who dares to take custody of ideas and notions meant for others. In some countries, Hoyte might be described as an autodidact. But in Trinidad he is not that far off from a madman. True, he is bad at what he does, but the fact that he is not in a position of power or privilege and has limited opportunities is discounted. The mockery is intensified when we consider how *Miguel Street* was originally published for the British market, a market that would view the world it describes as a remote, exotic place filled with "characters". Hoyte's industry becomes pretentious. He is a black man from a small island who does not know his place and is therefore to be laughed at.

But even a stopped clock is right twice a day. What is fiction if not an exercise in the power of ideas to conjure worlds? One human mind building a world and sharing that world through language? As Derrida might ask, what is language if not a medium by which the world is engendered? What is poetry if not an event in the world that also shapes the world? Titus Hoyte might be crazy, but his questions are not.

There's a Walcott poem, too, that sends me down the rabbit hole of imagined worlds and alternative realities. It's the untitled poem that closes his last collection, *White Egrets.* It begins:

This page is a cloud between whose fraying edges
a headland with mountains appears brokenly
then is hidden again until what emerges
from the now cloudless blue is the grooved sea

Just as Schopenhauer asks us to imagine the world being generated by an idea, Walcott asks us to commit to thoughts becoming solid in our hands. We look at the page, consider the poem's block of text. We are given a bird's eye view of a landscape, inhabiting the perspective of the titular white egrets of the book. The terrain unfurls: the colours of the land, the shapes of valleys, the curves of roads, the serenity of fishing villages. This is not just a picturesque tour. These details allude to the great concerns of Walcott's oeuvre without explicitly stating them: history, nature, love. Each item is a symbol, pointing to myth as well as social context. The fishing villages are the setting for ancient odysseys as well as the industrial-colonial processes that shaped the Caribbean's history.

And here what is at first beautiful becomes dangerous. There are shadows stalking the land, the road coils like a snake. "A line of gulls has arrowed" suggesting an offensive, the Daphne du Maurier idea of birds turning on man, as well as the arrows of Amerindians fighting for survival. Time itself is pierced. Each turn of the poem ("a widening harbour", "a town with no noise", "streets growing closer") is a stop along the way in a journey that is both linear and metaphorical. When "ancestral canoes" appear it is as though an Amerindian vessel has been excavated. We have crossed over. By the time we arrive at the closing lines ("a cloud slowly covers the page and it goes / white again and the book comes to a close") we have been on a disorienting journey, travelling film-reel style through a country, through feelings ("white, silent surges"), through life and through ages. That the poem makes us think of the poetry book in our hands is not tangential to the theme of death that runs through the collection. For the poet is asking us to reflect on the place of objects in our lives and the relevance of objects in the afterlife.

Walcott simultaneously casts and breaks a spell: we succumb to the world of the poem, its lines and language but then the suspension of disbelief is broken. Suddenly there is a book in our hands. Poetry has seemingly engendered an object, the same object that provides its genesis. This is a return to the source of all poetry: the idea as the poet as a maker of things.

Throughout his long career, Walcott was coming closer and closer to the ideas he expresses here. The first version of this poem appeared in 2007 in *The New York Review of Books* under the heading, "This Page is a Cloud". But long before that, in "Codicil", published in 1965's *The Castaway*, Walcott writes of a "clouding, unclouding sickle moon / whitening this beach again like a blank page". The opening of 1973's autobiographical *Another Life* also gives us:

Verandas, where the page of the sea
are a book left open by an absent master
in the middle of another life–
I begin here again,
begin until this ocean's
a shut book...

Then in 1979's *The Star-Apple Kingdom* we get "The Sea Is History" where, "the ocean kept turning blank pages". The page is a metaphorical domain for landscape. But in 1987's "To Norline" a relationship ends and, "when some line on a page / is loved... it's hard to turn." The stakes have been raised: the object in our hands is made into part of the poem, not just an idea within it. By 1997's *The Bounty*, "cloud-pages close in amen" in response to a bequest.

This idea of the page as both a conjured and conjuring medium betrays the influence of Ted Hughes' "The Thought Fox" where Hughes places his pastoral scene on "this blank page where my fingers move" and all the imagery climaxes with the declaration: "The page is printed". Considering the latter poem's own allusions to other poems such as Hopkin's "The Windhover", Blake's "The Tyger", and Coleridge's "Frost at Midnight", Walcott's extension of the idea from page to book effortlessly suggests worlds within worlds, books within books, writers within writers. (Peter Gizzi's "A page, we become" from his 1998 poem "Ledger Domain" also betrays a similar influence.)

It is no accident that Walcott ends *White Egrets* with this poem. Through-out the collection he surmises it will be his last book. He may have at one stage envisioned the poem as his last published piece. When his collected poems, *The Poetry of Derek Walcott 1948 – 2013*, appeared in 2014, the poem brought down the curtain. (The exhilarating lagniappe of *Morning, Paramin*, an ekphrastic work co-published with Peter Doig was yet to come.)

By punctuating his life's work with this untitled poem, Walcott impli-cates us. He asks us the same questions Titus Hoyte does. Like a philoso-pher concerned with the relationship between ideas, language and reality, the poet uses the fraught process of reading to make us consider what is more real: language or what it describes? Life or death? A poet's words, or the book that has been placed in our hands? When we close that book, what has happened to the poet and his words? And what has happened to us? Do we see the world around us afresh, as if born again? Or has something in that world changed? What is art if not a bridge between worlds? In my fantasy life, these are the kinds of questions I imagine Naipaul and Walcott arguing about over drinks like two tipsy characters in a novel or a play.

NAIPAUL'S NIGHTMARE

V.S. Naipaul wrote dozens of books but not the one with the most startling revelation about his life – *The World Is What It Is*, written by Patrick French and published in 2008. It generated headlines around the world. *The Telegraph*: "Sir Vidia Naipaul admits his cruelty may have killed wife". The same paper, another report: "V.S. Naipaul, failing as a human being". *The Daily Mail:* "Misogyny, mistresses and sadism". *The Atlantic*: "Cruel and unusual". *The Economist*: "Naked ambition". All eyes were on Naipaul's treatment of his first wife, his penchant for using prostitutes, his confirmation of a longstanding affair with an Argentinian woman, and, apparently, a sadomasochistic streak. Yet, tucked away in the book is a secret that possibly changes everything about the way we should see Naipaul, a secret that might even hold the key to some of the conduct covered by the headlines.

Everybody has an opinion on V.S. Naipaul, it seems, but do we really know him? The same man who during his lifetime was described as the greatest writer of English prose, even by his enemies, was the man who dismissed Jane Austen, Charles Dickens, E.M. Forster, James Joyce and more. The same man who won every literature prize imaginable, including the Nobel, was the man who was seen as racist, misogynistic, homophobic. The writer, some of whose fiction, such as *A House for Mr Biswas*, achieved a sublime lyrical humanity, was the same man who authored scornful reportage, throwing one-sided barbs at developing countries. Over time, critical views of literary reputation naturally wax and wane. The response to Naipaul's novel *The Enigma of Arrival* flip-flopped dramatically during his lifetime. First described as "scarred by scrofula" by Derek Walcott and as a book without love by Salman Rushdie, it was later declared a "masterpiece" by the Nobel Prize committee. If Naipaul was a character in one of his novels we would be impressed, then confused by his complexity. Familiar yet unreachable, a Janus, a Jekyll and Hyde, a Dorian Grey – it is hard to see his real face. But the telling disclosure, that should not have been missed because it appears in the first fifty pages of French's book, provides us with an important piece of the puzzle.

When Naipaul was six or seven his family moved to a cool, shady valley

of forest and snakes. The place, to the north of Trinidad's capital, was
Petit Valley. It was yet another move for the Naipaul family and young
Vidia was distraught. His grandmother tried to ease the transition. She
told him how beautiful the new location was, how pleasing the big
trees would be. Petit Valley was an estate of three hundred acres. An
old colonial house stood on a green, forested hillside, surrounded by
fruit trees: oranges, shaddocks, cacao, nutmeg, avocado, tangerines,
mangoes. In this Eden, Vidia and his family lived in a separate, smaller
house with a veranda, lit by oil lamps. One night, a fire began at the
back of this wooden building. Vidia and his sister had to flee through
a dark patch of forest. The Petit Valley is, of course, fictionalised as
Shorthills in *A House for Mr Biswas*. V.S. Naipaul's younger sister, Savi,
has also written about this period in her memoir *The Naipauls of Nepaul
Street*. The chapter title of her account, "Heidi of the Tropics" conveys
her sense of the innocence of place and time.

According French's book, it was around this time the molestation began.

"I was myself subjected to some sexual abuse by an older cousin. I was
corrupted, I was assaulted," Naipaul tells his biographer. "It was done in a
sly terrible way and it gave me a hatred, a detestation of this homosexual
thing." We are told the molestation continued intermittently over the next
two or three years, usually in the area where the boys slept. The perpetrator
was a male cousin. Naipaul did not report it at the time or later:

> "It was an outrage, but it was not a defining moment. I was very young.
> This thing was over before I was ten. I was always coerced. Of course
> he was ashamed too, later. It happened to other cousins. I think it is
> part of Indian extended family life, which is an abomination in some
> ways, a can of worms… After an assault one is very ashamed – and then
> you realise it happened to almost everybody. All children are abused.
> All girls are molested at some stage. It is almost like a rite of passage"
> (p. 36).

French's interviews with Naipaul on this topic occurred in July and
September 2002, indicating that Naipaul had kept this secret for six
decades. I believe, contrary to Naipaul's attempt to brush the matter off as
simply incidental to Indian life, his characterization of these episodes as
abuse, assault and molestation, his clear sense of shame, and the repeated
nature of the violations over a prolonged period of time – whatever the
complexities of his unwillingness or not – all suggest the matter was far
from insignificant. I cannot believe he was not traumatised. There is
perhaps some evidence of this in one of the childhood ailments that
Naipaul suffered – terrifying asthma attacks.

As Faulkner said, "The past is never dead. It's not even past." Every
person who has been subject to child abuse has a unique response. Trauma

has an impact on the developing brain. Maltreated children sometimes grow up to become maltreating adults. Studies have linked child abuse to increased risk in later life of panic reactions, depression, anxiety, sexual dissatisfaction, promiscuity, stress, difficulty in controlling anger, intimate partner violence. A veiled cascade of response to a violation that is, because of its nature, hidden from view.

Naipaul always had a troubled relationship with Trinidad. Two years after the abuse ended he resolved to leave. He did. He fled by gaining a scholarship to Oxford. What was he trying to leave behind? Did he continue to carry whatever it was with him? At Oxford, he suffered a mental breakdown which, according to his first editor Diana Athill, involved some form of unspeakable horror which he never specified. But though Naipaul would later write of Trinidad in disparaging terms, it was a place he could never escape, a place he always returned to in his fiction, reportage, and in making regular returns to see his family, as we learn from Savi Akal-Naipaul's memoir.

One of these returns was in 2007, five years after unburdening himself to French. When he visited his old college, he broke down in tears. When he was interviewed by the pro-vice chancellor of the local university, he cried. Elsewhere, he was irritable, intemperate, arrogant, cruel. It was all familiar behaviour. (The *Chicago Tribune,* in a headline, had once asked: "Why is V.S. Naipaul so cranky?") I believe his famous prickliness in interviews, his querulous, harried demeanour, his pompous smugness were not merely attributable to a Trinidadian cantankerousness or propensity for the teasing mischief of picong. It was, rather, a state not inconsistent with being a victim of child abuse. Naipaul's disposition towards Trinidad and his resultant worldview (in which he heaped scorn on similarly less-developed nations), and his emotional breakdowns on returning to his birthplace, whether literally or in his writing, were all signs of someone being triggered by inner stress.

"I never want to go through my childhood again," Naipaul told film-maker Adam Low, though the aspects of his childhood that he chose to fictionalise in *A House for Mr Biswas* were the state of virtual homelessness and domestic disorder until the family's arrival at Sikkim/Nepaul Street.

Jeremy Taylor has rightly observed, "Naipaul had to escape what he felt had been a nightmare childhood". That impulse to leave was not just the practical impulse felt by a generation of Windrush writers who sought opportunities in Britain. Interviewed by Derek Walcott in Trinidad in 1965, Naipaul said, "I find this place very frightening. I think this is a very sinister place." He was talking about what he saw as the damaging proletarianisation of Trinidadian life and culture, and no doubt alluding to the racial tribalism of the island. But such class warfare and racial strife are not unique to Trinidad. The intensity of his horror ("very frightening", "very sinister") indicates there was more in the mortar than the pestle.

Facts can be realigned, Naipaul once said, but fiction never lies. It reveals the writer totally. Inevitably, his crystalline prose laid bare his mental turmoil, even if a major source of the neurosis remained hidden. If abuse triggers abuse, it's possible to see his treatment of his characters in a new light.

For example, in *Guerillas*, a book that imposes inventions over a true story, the complexity of the main female character is erased. Robert Hemenway finds her to be "savagely portrayed", while Karl Miller notes "the novel breathes a certain animus" against her. Worse, the narrative adopts a fatalistic tone to her brutal murder. As much as we'd like to believe Naipaul is applying a journalistic approach to the thinly disguised real-life events behind the story, it's equally possible to argue he is throwing up the idea of Jane's fate being a form of justice because of failings and self-deceptions in her character. In other words, victim-shaming by innuendo. Perhaps tellingly, anal sex is framed as a special kind of degradation. And a child being raped becomes part of an elaborate fantasy dreamed up by a male protagonist, Jimmy Ahmed.

In *A Bend in the River,* Salim, a frequenter of female prostitutes in brothels, grows fond of sex that is "full of deliberate brutality", and in one scene beats a woman before having sex with her. In *Half a Life* there is talk of the fingering then rape of little girls. In *Magic Seeds*, a woman begs the main character to use a belt on her.

"Why does Naipaul create such scenes?" Robert Hemenway asks. The answer is possibly this: he was perpetually mirroring his abuse and its effects.

By way of contrast, in Naipaul's biggest and most autobiographical book, *A House for Mr Biswas,* written relatively early at the age of 29, the attention given to the sexual lives of characters is relatively paltry. The novel's artistic structure focuses on the figure of the father, Mr Biswas; this in itself guarantees that the novel does not deal with any latent sexual issues relating to the son, Anand. If there was suppression here, later work suggests that, as time passed, the need to revisit the Petit Valley's abuse gradually irrupted in the writing. Consider this moment from "A Flag in the Island" (1967), Naipaul's story about a former US marine ashore in Trinidad, in which the narrative suddenly ruptures, with a reflection on the terrors of childhood:

> This is part of my mood; it heightens my anxiety; I feel the whole world being washed away and that I am being washed away with it. I feel my time is short. The child, testing his courage, steps into the swiftly moving stream, and though the water does not go above his ankles, in an instant

the safe solid earth vanishes and he is aware only of the terror of sky and trees and the force at his feet" (pp. 479-480).

Naipaul's conflict when it comes to the factual details of his life mirrors these undercurrents. Torn, he vacillated between outwardly stating his distaste for writing an autobiography and actually writing such an autobiography under the permissive guise of fiction. Indeed, he was praised for blurring the line between autobiography and fiction, for pushing the novel to its limits, such as in his Booker prizewinning *In A Free State.* Still, even when he turned from the pretences of storytelling to reportage on the factual world, we get glimmers of his trauma. Murder will out. Here is Naipaul's description, in his first travel book, *The Middle Passage,* of making a return voyage to Trinidad:

> I began to feel my old fear of Trinidad. I did not want to stay... When I was in the fourth form I wrote a vow on the endpaper of my Kennedy's *Revised Latin Primer* to leave within five years. I left after six; and for many years afterwards in England, falling asleep in bedsitters with the electric fire on, I had been awakened by the nightmare that I was back in tropical Trinidad. (pp. 33-34)

Consider, too, this disclosure from his preface to *An Area of Darkness*:

> I was saved by the deeper anxiety that had been with me throughout the journey to India. This anxiety was that after *A House for Mr Biswas* I had run out of fictional material and that life was going to be very hard for me in the future; perhaps the writing career would have to stop. This anxiety took various forms, some mental, some physical, some a combination of the two. The most debilitating anxiety was that I was losing the gift of speech. It was at the back of everything I did. (p.6)

Often, in works of art, such as Alfred Hitchcock's film, *Rope* (1948), what appears to be one kind of story turns out to be a code for something else. In the case of that film the criminal enterprise at its heart is a cipher for homosexuality. In a similar way, Naipaul's intense anxieties, which he attributed to a fear of his writing career coming to an end, point not just to the precarious nature of a creative life, they point to a past that held sway over him. This past, this trauma, migrated to his fiction, influenced his political views, shaped the attitudes expressed in his non-fiction and interviews. I believe the trauma also bled into his private life and his relations with people. Even the author's seemingly innocuous choice of a home in the green and leafy countryside of Wiltshire, described hypnotically in *The Enigma of Arrival*, was a return to the verdant site of an inescapable wounding, a movement away from the urban landscape of London to the countryside, a repeat of his family's temporary retreat from the densely-packed suburb of Woodbrook to the hills to the north of Port of Spain.

But is this too simple? Too novelistic, even? It's no doubt unwise to try to reduce entire lives to a single set of motivations, impulses and events. And why didn't French, Naipaul's own biographer, make more of the disclosures in *The World Is What It Is*? The biographer spends one page out of five-hundred on the matter, then moves on. We get the feeling the incident was written off as perhaps nothing more than experimentation of some sort, or an affirmation of the old adage, "boys will be boys".

Yet, to isolate a single thread is not to present a simplistic solution to this riddle. It is to tease out the complexity of the overall writing personality. And there is a lot of complexity.

For instance, what are we to make of Naipaul's views on women writers? On the one hand he could declare, "I read a piece of writing and within a paragraph or two I know whether it is by a woman or not." On the other hand, this is a writer who openly professed to relying heavily on the judgment of women to produce his own books. Everything he wrote was first read by his wives. At his first publisher, where he published his early masterworks, he was edited by a woman. Publicly he could dismiss Jane Austen as being an example of her class: a female writer having a "sentimental view of the world", while behind closed doors he subjected his manuscripts to vetting by the women closest to him. Naipaul's treatment of queerness, too, is similarly contradictory.

Naipaul was not really on my gaydar as I grew up gay in Trinidad. I only began to take a closer look after he won the Nobel Prize in 1992 and after reading his short story "Tell Me Who To Kill".

We turn to literature both to see the world, and to see ourselves. As a child I turned to representations of gay characters in all mediums. I looked for independent verification, for corroboration and affirmation of my own dignity. I was drawn to something in "Tell Me Who To Kill", even if I was not yet to understand it fully. The handling of the material, the characters – it was all suffused with an aura of innuendo and implication surrounding the relationship between the male narrator and his friend, Frank. We get the sense we are reading the germ of a novel. There is no real story. The piece is more about mood. Its journey is cinematographic, its tone film noir. There are surreal flashbacks, scenes of peril and dread. This is intensified by the presence, the ghost perhaps, of the real-life story of two Trinidadian Indian brothers who, not long before Naipaul wrote the story between August 1969 and October 1970, became infamous for a murder. The details of the case of Arthur and Nizamodeen Hosein were darkly comic (except to the unfortunate murdered woman and her family); they kidnapped the wrong person, according to trial prosecutors. Naipaul's story does not exploit that kind of tragic absurdity, but he very probably drew on the trial narrative of the picture of influence and dependence between the Hosein brothers. Into the mix must also be added the possibility that Naipaul reflected and drew upon his troubled relationship with his younger brother Shiva. Through all of the fog, the narrator's strong quasi-homosexual bond with his white friend, Frank, stands out:

> Frank touch me on the arm. I am glad he touch me, but I shrug his hand away. I know it isn't true, but I tell myself he is on the other side, with the others, looking at me without looking at me. I know it isn't true about Frank because, look, he too is nervous. He want to be alone with me; he don't like being with his own people. It isn't like being on a bus or in a café, where he can be like a man saying: I protect this man with me. (p. 99)

The story ends just before a wedding, but it is not a celebration of the homosexual couple. On the contrary, by its concluding line, which makes reference to *Rope*, the piece has followed a long homophobic tradition of linking queerness to mental instability and criminality.

The more I read Naipaul, the more I found signs of a curiosity about and concern for gay characters, though the gay characters who appear within the folds of his narratives are not fleshed out and granted the complexity of real people – and are invariably served tragic ends.

So Bobby in *In a Free State* is humiliated, denuded, his face rubbed against the floor, his wrist broken by soldiers. Alan in *The Enigma of Arrival* dies of a drug overdose.

In *Guerillas,* Bryant goes crazy, Jimmy *is* crazy. They become murderers. Conforming to the stereotype of queerness being pitted against masculinity, Leonard Side in *A Way in the World* is described as a "decorator of cakes" who works "all his life with flowers". We are introduced to him as a man, "doing things to a dead body on a table or slab in front of him" with "hairy fingers". He falls ill. We never learn if he survives this illness; the nebulous implication is death could well have been his fate. This is a work of fiction but his character is apparently not even deserving of that kind of basic resolution. A school teacher, whose only function in the book is to tell us about Leonard, describes Leonard thus: "He frightened me because I felt his feeling for beauty was like an illness; as though some unfamiliar, deforming virus had passed through his simple mother to him" (pp. 7-8).

In the Caribbean and in many parts of the world still hostile to LGBTQ rights, homosexuality is maliciously and simplistically linked to paedophilia and child abuse. Did Naipaul make that link in his mind? Could this explain his homophobia? His dismissal of E.M. Forster and John Maynard Keynes as nasty homosexuals?

Or, given how Naipaul's generation dealt with homosexuality, could Naipaul himself have had a more complex relationship with the idea of same-sex desire? Is it possible that his own homophobia was to some extent the expression of internalised conflict, directed at nascent tendencies, tendencies which then triggered shame and self-loathing and the desire to violently squash the legitimacy of such feelings?

I hold no brief for Naipaul's homophobia. I don't think it can be justified or excused. Instead, I want to ask questions. I want to observe, as was observed of Hamlet's mother, that Naipaul doth protest too much.

Some years after Naipaul's discussion with his biographer, his sister Kamla, who held his hand in Petit Valley the night they ran through the forest from the fire, confirmed that Naipaul had never spoken to her about the abuse.

"I didn't know about this. Because if I did I would have been mad like hell. I would have been extremely annoyed. Nothing was told to me," she said to *Newsday*. Like many others, she did not think the experience affected her brother's life.

"He's not easily worried by something like that," she said. But is it really possible not to be "worried by something like that"? Naipaul's sensitivity is legendary. For instance, he famously declined to read his own letters to his father, even when they were being collated for publication.

"Certain things are so painful one prefers not to be reminded of them," Naipaul told broadcaster Charlie Rose. Is it really possible to assume that a person, who could become paralysed at the thought of reading correspondence from his earlier life, could simply turn off the tap when it came to his experience of child abuse?

Not only did Naipaul manifest the lingering effects in his writing, people around him knew something was up.

"Vidia's anxiety and despair were real: you need only compare a photograph of his face in his twenties with one taken in his forties to see how it had been shaped by pain," wrote Athill in her famous *Granta* essay on editing Naipaul. "It was my job to listen to his unhappiness and do what I could to ease it – which would not have been too bad if there had been anything I *could* do."

Something of this anxiety and despair stalks the writing. It's channelled in "Tell Me Who to Kill" where, as noted, Naipaul suffuses the story with the doom and gloom of *Rope*. He punctuates the narrative with a dazzling array of film references that perform key functions in the narrative. Consider the first mention of a film; it helps us build a psychological profile of the narrator:

> And it is as though you are frightened of something it is bound to come, as though because you are carrying danger with you danger is bound to come. And again it is like a dream. I see myself in this old English house, like something in *Rebecca* starring Laurence Oliver and Joan Fountain. It is an upstairs room with a lot of jalousies and fretwork. No weather. I am there with my brother, and we are strangers in the house. (p. 62)

The film version of Daphne du Maurier's novel *Rebecca* is a love story that follows a woman who marries a man, only to find out that she will always be in the shadow of his first wife who died in mysterious circumstances. The reference to fretwork and jalousies is a refraction of the gingerbread houses of Trinidad from which the narrator originates. Importantly, *Rebecca* is a film featuring many twists and turns and sinister elements that conspire to deceive and smother the woman. The sense of unseen danger, of helplessness, may be transposed to Naipaul's protagonist. Houses are always important symbols, particularly from the author of *A House for Mr Biswas*, but the line, "we are strangers in the house" echoes the title of another suspenseful Hitchcock film, *Strangers on a Train* (1951), where two men plot murder. In this story, another early film reference shows how the protagonist has used movies to map London's urban landscape. His vision of what the city is supposed to look like has come partially from *Waterloo Bridge*, named after the famous bridge off the Strand:

> I used to have a vision of a big city. It wasn't like this, not streets like this. I used to see a pretty park with high black iron railings like spears, old thick trees growing out of the wide pavement, rain falling the way it fall over Robert Taylor in *Waterloo Bridge*, and the pavement covered with flat leaves of a perfect shape in pretty colours, gold and red and crimson. (p. 72)

Waterloo Bridge (1940) is a noirish film about a ballerina who kills herself. All of the films feature characters in love or with secrets or both, and these secrets in different ways threaten to engulf and destroy them. This is true of *Jesse James* (1939), and, very true of *Rope*, which dominates the short story. In an extended fantasy sequence, the narrator imagines something tragic happening, something which must be concealed and covered up by him and by his beloved, his brother, Dayo. As with most Hitchcock films, this tragic incident appears to come out of nowhere and embroils an ordinary person who must move from a banal situation into one of extraordinary peril. In a dream sequence, the narrator takes us to a place somewhere proximate to the house in *Rebecca* and tells us of "a quarrel, a friendly argument, a scuffle" involving a friend of Dayo that results in a murder. The details are only telegraphed; we learn the boys "are only playing, but the knife go in the boy, easy." The narrator says:

And the body is in the house, in a chest, like in *Rope* with Fairley Granger. It is there at the beginning, it is there forever, and everything else is only like a mockery. But we eat. My brother is trembling; he is not a good actor. The people we are eating with, I can't see their faces, I don't know what they look like. (pp. 62-63)

The second *Rope* reference occurs with the reappearance of "Fairley Granger" – or Farley Granger – whose hairstyle is compared to Dayo's. Then the imagined encounter with the friend of Dayo – now described as a college friend – recurs and again death comes. Again when a penetrating knife goes in, "it is an accident" and, "The body is in the chest, like in *Rope*, but in this English house." The entire story ends, in film-reel fashion, with a panoramic sweep of several images that have dotted the narrative and a fourth and final reference to *Rope*:

I have my own place to go back to. Frank will take me there when this is over. And now that my brother leave me for good I forget his face already, and I only seeing the rain and the house and the mud, the field at the back with the pará-grass bending down with the rain, the donkey and the smoke from the kitchen, my father in the gallery and my brother in the room on the floor and that boy opening his mouth to scream, like in *Rope*. (pp. 107-108)

All these ciphers, all these codes hang over "Tell Me Who to Kill", giving powerful weight to the unnamed narrator's heart-breaking declaration: "I only know that inside me mash up, and that the love and danger I carry all this time break and cut, and my life finish." As he considers his past and his alienated present there is no fighting spirit as suggested by the title. Instead, traumatised, he declares, "I am the dead man."

I once attended an event in Trinidad to commemorate Derek Walcott. Members of the audience were invited to ask questions. In posing a question, someone mentioned Naipaul's name. Immediately there was a noisy uproar. It became clear that the mere mention of his name can still trigger strong emotions. I saw a similar thing when, weeks later, I chaired a discussion panel at the Bocas Lit Fest on Naipaul in downtown Port of Spain. Some people strongly defend him. Others excoriate him. None can ignore him.

Reading his work it's easy to see why he is revered. It's also easy to see why he is hated. It's not just the misogyny and the homophobia. It's the scathing, one-sided, selective attacks often directed at the disadvantaged, the marginal, the black, the brown. It's the overall feeling of disdain. It's his condescension, the aroma and suggestion of his own superiority, his surprise at any sort of achievement by others whom he regards as lesser. It seems the wilful inversion of what we expect writers to do. We expect writers, we expect journalists, to hold the powerful to account. But Naipaul tells us, "The world is what it is; men who are nothing, who allow themselves to become nothing, have no place in it". This monstrous fatalism, which is at odds with the feeling and warmth of his early masterpiece, *Biswas*, cannot be exorcised through any simple formula.

But it can be complicated. By this complication, by this admission into the evidence of his own frailty, we can restore curmudgeonly Naipaul to the type of complexity he so zealously denied many of his subjects. We can restore the little boy who once held his sister's hand as they ran together through Petit Valley away from a house on fire. Everybody has an opinion on V.S. Naipaul but, in the end, can we ever really know him?

ON HENRY JAMES

The Turn of the Screw

THE

remark   was

strange

The

house

dreadful

It was

evening

that same evening,

he brought out what was in

his pockets.

7

THE TURN OF THE SCREW

his eyes

his hand

his
locked drawer

ice,
silence.

'Then your manuscript -?'

dead
died

8

THE TURN OF THE SCREW

he

was

the

most

beautiful

garden

struck me

told me

I could see.

came out

coming out.

light.

9

MARK TWAIN'S CORN-PONE OPINIONS

Years of thought and debate have gone into the monumental question and yet it's still to be answered: Is there a difference between corn-pone and corn bread? And is corn-pone cooked in a skillet or baked? Should it have sugar, milk and eggs? Should it have baking soda? Is corn-pone one word or two? There are no such difficulties, however, when it comes to distinguishing corn-pone, whatever that is, from what is called, in Trinidad, pone.

Trinidad pone is a delicious, delectable dessert, a confection carefully crafted from cassava, coconut, sugar and spice. It's sold everywhere: to hoity-toity hipsters in uppity farmers' markets; to starving bachelors at no-frill vegetable stalls; to momzillas in bakeries on the main street; to old tanties in parlours on the corner; to blue-collar workers shopping in supermarket chains, and to smily-faced children in tiny school cafes. I've had "gourmet" pone, from a restaurant that specialises in "deconstructed local classics". I've had pone from a tired lady selling snacks to raise funds for her sick son. I've had pone warm, lightly drizzled with a caramel sauce. I've eaten it cold, as if it were some kind of iced treat, on the warm sands of the northern coast.

Pone is made of cassava but if you're not a purist (and want to be wrong) there's leeway as to what you can put in it. Some people use pumpkin to add excitement to their life by raising the colour of the dish. That colour tends to fall somewhere along a spectrum between pale brown to golden. The texture of pone, however, is consistently the same: gelatinous Turkish delight cocooned in a crisp cassava coconut skin. Connoisseurs of taste add loads of ground spice: cinnamon, nutmeg, ginger and cloves. The raucous and more adventurous throw in raisins, but this is universally accepted to be a gratuitous touch.

Trinidad pone isn't to be confused with Jamaican pone, which is, unfortunately, made from sweet potato, milk, sugar, and rum. Incidentally, the overbearingly lumpy Jamaican pone is at times made from cornmeal and is as ostentatious as a dancehall queen. The Jamaican use of cornmeal makes the theory that Caribbean pone is the sweeter, better-looking brother to the American pone seem plausible.

Yet, for all these nuances, Trinidadians feel no need for precision. A

Trinidadian will call cassava pone "pone", removing the adjective in the assumption that what constitutes pone here must also be pone everywhere. In fact, had I not encountered Mark Twain's famous essay, "Corn-pone Opinions", I might have never questioned what a pone is and how it differs from a bread. Nor would I have pondered the fact that some dictionaries say a corn-pone is a simple-minded person, a meaning which might have something to do with the argument in Twain's essay.

Twain isn't concerned with the complexities of pone aesthetics. He takes for granted that when he opens his essay with a slave saying, "You tell me whar a man gits his corn pone, en I'll tell you what his 'pinions is", we'll know what corn pone is and, what's more, that we'll understand its place in 1901 society. Admittedly, Twain didn't publish the essay in his lifetime – it was published posthumously in 1923. But Twain being dead hasn't stopped him from having still acclaimed work. His essay opens *The Best American Essays of the Century*, edited by Joyce Carol Oates.

Instead of a dessert, Twain has his sights on making a mundane point about the way people think, or rather, don't think. He believes his friend, the slave, is saying man is not independent and cannot afford views that might interfere with his bread and butter (to mix up the pone metaphor a bit). He also feels his friend is saying that in order to prosper we must all line up with the majority, must think and feel what everybody else thinks and feels, or else suffer the consequences.

"He must restrict himself to corn-pone opinions," Twain paraphrases. "He must get his opinions from other people; he must reason out none for himself; he must have no first-hand views."

Twain actually thinks the situation is more dire. Whereas his friend feels people cherry-pick their opinions strategically, Twain believes this exceeds their capabilities. Whereas his friend assumes it's possible to formulate original positions, Twain casts doubt on the existence of free thought. He says:

> I am persuaded that a coldly-thought-out and independent verdict upon a fashion in clothes, or manners, or literature, or politics, or religion, or any other matter that is projected into the field of our notice and interest, is a most rare thing – if it has ever existed.

To wit, the only way people could like hideous hoop skirts was because everyone else did.

When I was a wee child, I was a well-behaved Trinidadian boy. I listened to my parents. I went to church. I tried to become an acolyte (though they threw me out after suspecting I was more into the pretty, flowing gowns that the Holy Ghost). I paid attention in school. Back then, the Belmont Boys Roman Catholic School was yet to develop a reputation for bad boys and ruffians. I studied hard. By Standard Five, however, this good behaviour started to get me into trouble. As everyone knows, there is only so much good behaviour that little boys can take. The other boys grumbled, softly at first, then openly, that I had never made a mark in the world, had never distinguished myself through any form of truancy, had neglected to uphold the long-held tradition of boys being in fights. Such was my appalling lack of decency and civic-mindness, that the elder boys were incensed. I became a pariah, a figure of censure, *persona non grata*.

To address this misconduct, it behoved me to take action. I arranged, with another similarly-circumstanced do-gooder to orchestrate a skirmish. We discussed our plan, and scheduled an appropriate day for the momentous duel. Naivety got the better of us: we believed it necessary to come up with a background story to justify our war. A jumbled narrative involving the theft of marbles and a lunch kit in which a precious piece of pone had been stolen was formulated and tantalisingly teased out. There was enough withholding of key details to fan the flames of speculation and conjecture. Then, the Friday of our chosen appointment arrived. We wanted tales of our exploits to spread over the weekend.

The school bell rang like a death knell. I immediately pushed around Kwesi for a while; he grabbed the neck of my shirt; I ripped off a button or two of his, as we groaned and grunted strenuously as a mark of our manly exertions. The fight needed to have an epic scale so we prolonged it for as long as possible until, both of us having run out of moves, it came to a natural end. It was determined – universally I think – that the fight was a good one, that we both had "won" since there was little to distinguish us, though maybe Kwesi had a few more scratches on his arm than I did.

So when Mark Twain alludes to the ridiculous lengths people will endure in order to conform, I fully understand.

And I think it's safe to say everyone has had that moment when there's a new emperor and he's not wearing clothes, but you have to pretend he is, and not only do you have to pretend he is but you also have to compliment him on just how fabulous the clothes are, even if you're seeing nothing. You do it because everyone else is complimenting him and if you don't people will think you are dumb or blind or just plain mean. The Emperor's New Clothes explains the success of many films, books, plays, and art exhibitions. Entire careers have been built on work that is, even within the subjective realm of the humanities, unlikeable, but which has nonetheless found favour with people, or at least been *said* to have found favour with people – the snowball growing bigger and bigger, threatening to squash anyone who will not yield. Twain was onto something.

Social media has magnified this. It's given us tools by which we can empirically gauge just how admired something is, how many views it has received, the quantum of votes it has drawn or comments it has acquired. Some of us, seeing only that other people have liked something, sheepishly click the like button without reading the full post, or listening to the full podcast, or watching the full twenty-minute video.

But when Twain's nameless slave, whom we will call Uncle Jake, says "You tell me whar a man gits his corn pone, en I'll tell you what his 'pinions is", what Uncle Jake truly means is not what Twain hears. What Uncle Jake was alluding to was the unabashed fact that people are generally self-serving. We all have vested interests, hidden agendas, values that fall to the wayside if there is a need to ensure self-preservation. People do not consider deontological values, as a philosopher might say, nor do they care about the greater utilitarian good; we cannot afford such luxuries when living from day to day, meal to meal, pay cheque to pay cheque. This *does* assume the capacity for independent thinking. But the premise is not the conclusion.

Nor is it worth attacking that premise. For the assertion of self-preservation is selfish, sovereign thinking. What is more independent than that?

Is Twain really sceptical about the possibility of free thought? If there is no independent thought in the world, this would make his corn-pone opinions axiomatic. We would live in a deterministic world. There would be no choices on the menu. What would be the point of saying someone has an opinion? We would all have a passion for hoop skirts come hell or high water.

But even if Twain's interpretation of Uncle Jake's proverb is substantially correct, I have reservations about his argument.

"We are creatures of outside influences," he argues; "as a rule we do not think, we only imitate." However even when we copy, we mentally formulate our positions. We decide, consciously or even subconsciously, whether we will follow the status quo. Twain underestimates how much we *intuit*.

All this cogitation on corn-pone opinions makes one have a hankering for corn-pone itself. But what exactly does it taste like? As Tom Sawyer did before me, I steal into the kitchen. Call it research. Call it art. Call it hunger. Why shouldn't I indulge my taste buds? I devise a plan. I assess the stocks in my pantry, pull out my smart phone, and scour the internet for recipes. This throws up the first challenge. The search yields a million results.

Corn-pone is so popular there must be a reason. It's clearly been around for a long time. The internet tells me it's a Native American dish, corn being primarily a Native American invention. (Interestingly, Trinidad's pone, made from cassava, has also been linked to our indigenous peoples.)

My chosen recipe calls for just five things: cornmeal, water, milk, salt, and baking powder. I'm not sure about the baking powder though. Wouldn't the more authentic corn-pone be flat and unleavened? Did people always have baking powder to hand when roving through the forest, pitching tents, lighting fires and whatnot?

I halve the recipe. Don't really need four corn-pones for this experiment when two will suffice. Listed are precise measurements to follow, but I've got a deft hand so I go with the flow, eyeing the amounts I put it. Cooking is a science but it's also an art. You use what's to hand, you do what feels right, drawing from experience.

Just as meals are fashioned in this intuitive way, so too do we formulate viewpoints. We are not machines. We do not always think things through, yes, but at the same time we feel. We intuit and, therefore, we reason.

The corn meal is a light dusty yellow, but when I add my liquid ingredients the colour gets deeper – more saffron than butternut, more turmeric than lemon. It comes together in a dough that's similar to the dough we use in Trinidad to make Christmas pastelles, a kind of stuffed polenta; a steamed empanada. As I knead the dough, which feels like the plasticine children used to amuse themselves with, feels as real as thoughts made material, I think about how easy it is to forget the past, forget the names of all the tribes and peoples who might have done the same thing. Yet we are still tied to them. A simple thing like a meal can be a commemoration.

Our very nature is to feel. Feeling allows us to sense whether we think something is morally sound. Our emotions guide us. This is a kind of reason. Without having a principle clearly formulated in our minds, we know something is bad just by the way we feel. Stealing. Killing. Lying. We talk of conscience. Even if something is the bees knees, we first have to decide if it tickles our fancy. Hoop skirts only became the rage because they pleased us on a level we may not have been able to articulate.

Sometimes, the results of this process are dangerous: the wrong emotions dominate. So it is fear that accounts for the rise of the Nazis, the racism of Twain's America, the xenophobia of Britain. The Brexit vote, the rise of Donald Trump have emboldened certain people to come out and follow suit. The cause: fear. People are afraid of that most reliable of boogeymen: The Other. The counter to such fear is to draw upon opposite and equally powerful emotions: compassion, love, kindness. Understanding that we are all human. For things to change, these purer feelings must be admitted into the equation.

My pones are surprisingly satisfying. I try them with butter. I try them with maple syrup. I try cheese. They are like arepas. They can match whatever you put on them, meet flavours halfway.

But let's say Twain is right and all we do is conform. Can't conforming still be a form of resistance? Can't it trigger rebellion? Be it's own sign of an independent assertion of values?

When Rosa Parks got onto the bus at Montgomery, Alabama, on December 1, 1955, she didn't disobey any rules. She conformed to them. The prevailing laws divided the bus into white and black sections. Parks sat in the black section. When the white section filled up, the bus driver attempted to expand the section for whites-only. The law called for "equal but separate accommodations". It didn't permit this practice of shifting the goalpost, a practice that had apparently developed over time. Parks stayed in the section designated for her under the law. She said: "When that white driver stepped back toward us, when he waved his hand and ordered us up and out of our seats, I felt a determination cover my body like a quilt on a winter night." It was by conforming to a racist law that she asserted her individuality. It was through this conforming that she defied everything. If individuals could find freedom through compliance, so too could entire nations.

In the mid-twentieth century, a wave swept through the Caribbean. Territories of the British Empire sought what Rosa Parks achieved. They flirted with, lobbied for, then gained independence. Jamaica and Trinidad and Tobago in 1962, Barbados and Guyana in 1966, Bahamas in 1973, Grenada in 1974, Suriname in 1975, Dominica in 1978, St. Lucia in 1979, St. Vincent in 1979, Belize and Antigua and Barbuda in 1981, St. Kitts and Nevis in 1983. One by one, they attained access to the comity of nations.

Was this wave merely a case of follow fashion? Or was swimming with the tide a way of swimming against it? By emulating each other's example, these countries cultivated the sense of a shared destiny. This made the fate of the islands irresistible. In this way, independence was achieved not through bloody rebellion, but through collective power. There was strength in numbers. As swimmers in the Caribbean will tell you, to survive a deadly current, sometimes you must let it take you, then slowly make your way to the shore.

"Power is everywhere," wrote Michel Foucault, "not because it embraces everything, but because it comes from everywhere." We see power in action when individuals protest peacefully. We see it when nations come together to raise a fist. We also see it when artists, painters, musicians, writers, and poets adopt forms that, on the surface, seem like imitations but, in truth, are signals of resistance.

St Lucian poet Derek Walcott and gay poet Thom Gunn did this. They sometimes put on a costume, paraded in it, then took it off in order to move on to the next poem, or sequence or book. In their verse, these poets set out to show that they too could write in the traditional forms that have dominated English letters for centuries. Walcott took on the idea of the epic, its rhythms, tones and textures. He co-opted the theatre, emulating Shakespeare, and produced dramas in verse. He applied these forms not to white, European subjects, but to the Caribbean. His mimicking was not appeasement. It was an assertion of a black man's inherent and equal claim to words. "The English language is nobody's special property," he said.

Like Walcott, Gunn was a poet with a penchant for the metres of a long tradition. His poems followed a regimented pulse. Sonnets, elegies, syllabic verse, couplets. Yet, using these forms Gunn addressed the queer, even when carefully wrapped and tied with a metaphorical bow. The poem, "The Allegory of the Wolf Boy", is about life as a gay adolescent. Like Walcott, he too was laying down the gauntlet on behalf of a disenfranchised class. "Rebellion," Gunn wrote, "comes dressed in conformity".

These poets know what Twain forgets. Twain underestimates how following can be leading. It can be the ultimate inside job.

Corn-pone opinions reflecting the general consensus might appear shallow, simplistic, half-baked. But that alone should not stop us from taking a second good bite.

DOUBLES

Not the tennis game but the internationally acclaimed street food from Trinidad. A thing of contradiction. Deep-fried and hearty, yet totally vegan. Soft, delicate, yet solid and meaty. Neatly wrapped for eaters on the go, yet messy, drenched in finger-licking deliciousness. One word, both singular and plural – like barracks, binoculars, shorts. Seemingly everywhere, but available only at certain times and certain places. Mornings and nights. Never in restaurants, always at roadsides, under tents, or off mobile carts – Trinidad's version of the trendy food truck.

Some people say the main ingredient is chickpeas or channa. It's an ingredient that harks to a history predating the dish itself. Chickpeas were found in places of power and reverence, buried with Egyptian mummies from 6000 BC. The Greeks, according to Plato, ate them with figs for dessert, and the Romans made dishes from them as offerings to the goddess of love. Pliny the Elder reportedly called the chickpea "the pea of Venus", and a physician to emperor Marcus Aurelius believed that chickpeas increased sperm count. The sexiness of the pea may have something to do with the fact that it looks like a butt – something which could explain its popularity among Trinidadians, though few biting into a doubles are aware that its main ingredient helped change the world. The chickpea was an affordable source of protein in ancient Rome; its cultivation supplemented the diet of subsistence farmers. In this way, the pea, the size of a very small coin, helped sustain the Roman Empire.

There are people who say the main ingredient of doubles is the bara, the bread, the deep-fried bake, the fried flatbread, between which the channa is sandwiched. In the Bible, the Hebrew word *bara* (meaning to shape, fashion, create) appears seventeen times in Isaiah, eight times in Genesis and six times in the Psalms. When used with God as the active subject, it means to make heaven and earth, to birth man, to engender something new, to bring about a miracle. Many hungry bellies will agree about doubles' miraculous qualities in the morning. But bara has other meanings – to cut down or cut out. It also means to make yourself fat, which again is appropriate.

Yet other people say the main ingredient of doubles is not an ingredient, but the sauces. If the humble chickpea propped up empires, empires conspired, through the march of history, to give us the toppings for our doubles. The mango, that relative of the cashew, came, like the curry used in the channa, from India. It lends a sweetness to complement the savoury. Indigenous peoples of the Americas bestowed the shadon beni, a more intense cousin to cilantro with serrated leaves and blue flowers. The tamarind, from Africa, was brought to the Americas, along with slaves, by the Spanish who, like us, enjoyed its bittersweet tartness. And then there's pepper, an ingredient whose nuances are so complex to the average Trinidadian it would take an entire book to discuss. But with regard to doubles and pepper, one thing is clear. When requesting "slight" pepper from a vendor, the novice should be aware there will be no real difference between "slight" and the full dose of fire. To be thorough we must also mention the humble cucumber, also from India and also ancient. It appears in the legends of Gilgamesh and in Numbers in the Bible, before ending up as a savoury topping at Ariapita Avenue.

The consumption of doubles is a barometer of society. When the economy is healthy, robust vendors spring up like mushrooms after rain, congregating at night in hives near popular watering holes, capitalising on the flow of inebriated citizens looking for something to hit the spot after a night of excess. When the economy is going even better, "gourmet" doubles appear – stuffed with unorthodox ingredients like cheese, chicken and beef – things no proper doubles connoisseur would ordinarily want or need. But such are the ways of decadence. Economists, whenever tax revenue has fallen, call on governments to tax profligate doubles vendors.

The darker side of society also manifests itself around this meal. In 2012, a man was planassed with a cutlass while buying doubles. Crime, citizens said, was becoming intolerable. In 2014, three people tried to rob a doubles vendor after buying a meal. Crime, citizens said, was at an all-time high. In 2019, a doubles vendor was murdered at his doubles stand. Citizens said nothing.

I've heard stories about people stowing doubles in their carry-on luggage on long flights to gift hungry fans of the dish abroad. I've read accounts of people experimenting with the idea of freezing and shipping the bara and channa separately for reassembly elsewhere. I've yet to come across, however, anyone who makes doubles in their home. The recipe, involving a long process of allowing dough to rise, soaking dried beans overnight, then boiling them for a long time, then frying the bara over high temperatures, is too much even for domestic gods and goddesses. Which resonates with doubles' central contradiction: it is casually available on the streets yet in many ways is inaccessible. Its simplicity belies its reliance on the economies of scale and collective appetite. Its flavours and textures curdle into its own realm of enjoyment – a realm with a history and complexity as multitudinous as Trinidad itself.

Yet, Trinidadians treat doubles they way they treat their own. On an ordinary day, the fact of doubles selling at the side of the road is taken for granted. But when a foreign travel writer, famous internationally, films a documentary and reports on doubles as a unique "street food" and a "speciality", the doubles is suddenly back in vogue, restored to its status of being part of our national heritage. That heritage is at once as rich as it is contingent, layered as it is unstable, unique as it is universal, succulent as it is frail, innovative as it is stale.

IN PLATO'S CAVE

It was wrong, but as a kid I sided with the Nguyamyams. They were the citizens of the planet Pakaskas. Pakaskas had mountains made of jelly, houses made of donuts, roads made of rice-cakes, rivers of cream, and seas of molten chocolate. In this land of milk and honey, the Nguyamyams spent all their time eating. They didn't bother to think about building for the future or leaving leftovers for tomorrow.

Never heard of the Nguyamyams? I hadn't either until April 1992, when the United Nations (UN) released a short clay animation video for young children. In the film, which every Trinidadian of a certain vintage would have seen on television, a wise Nguyamyam named Inggolok issues a stark warning. He tells his fellow Nguyamyams their planet is disappearing. The greedy Nguyamyams don't listen. They continue to chew, savour and slurp away. Eventually, a defeated Inggolok leaves the planet. He travels with his family to a new world. On this new planet, he watches helplessly as planet Pakaskas, already half-devoured, is masticated into oblivion.

The UN had good intentions. The moral of the story was clear. We were supposed to come away with the need for environmental protection, resource conservation. We were supposed to understand that we should do no harm to the planet.

I got the opposite message.

I sided with the little green Nguyamyams. "Keep eating and when we've eaten up everything here, we'll just look for another planet," they said. "Go on, eat!" To a slightly chubby boy from Port of Spain with an ever-growing penchant for macaroni pie, pone, roti, and doubles, their hedonism was irresistible. Who could say no to all those carbs? Inggolok, whiny and annoying, was like the adult who tries to force you to eat your vegetables. I felt sorry for him and more sorry for his skinny children, taken away from all that butter cake, ice cream, and cotton candy.

I look back with horror at how I first viewed things. It's amazing how the same film can change as we change; how beauty is not the only thing in the eye of the beholder; how art can both instruct and be instructed by time. The mirror has two faces.

Nguyamyam was just one cinematographic landmark in my childhood. Another was *The Sound of Music*. I remember the day Father brought it home. There was a particular look on his face I'd seen many times before.

Whenever he came back from the video store he had it: a wide grin, excitement gleaming from one side of his face to the other. He seemed thrilled by the prospect of unleashing the latest masterpiece on us. Back in those days, people put on good clothes and lined the streets in downtown Port of Spain queuing to see a Disney release. *Beauty and the Beast. Aladdin.* Cinema was a simple, unadulterated joy. But then technology changed. Suddenly, you could bring the experience to your house. Father could get videotapes, whether rented, bought or however else procured, put them into the VCR, press play, and presto! Magic.

I don't remember watching the film the first time.

I remember watching it later that same day, that week, that month, that year, in the years following. It's safe to say there was an unhealthy addiction to it in our home. We'd neglect our chores and sit around the television under its spell. We could gallivant on the mountains with Julie Andrews, dance in the rain and sing about our favourite things, play with goat puppets, roam the streets of Salzburg wearing curtains. However, at each viewing the film would end at the same moment. Those familiar with the movie will recognise that moment. It's after Maria flees the house, returns to the Abbey, and confesses to the Mother Abbess her love for Captain von Trapp. Mother Abbess promptly begins to sing "Climb Every Mountain".

As children, it did not matter to us that we never knew if Maria married the Captain, nor what happened to the Baroness, nor what the significance of the Nazi flag and the Nazi officer wooing one of the girls was. It did not matter that the song never reached its zenith, was interrupted, crudely, by static noise, a strange and sudden moment of pixilated snow, before some other texture, some other film, over which *The Sound of Music* had been recorded, resumed. Those were the days before you could Google to find out the ending of a film.

The restrictions conditioned us. Here was this movie that we now owned. (If it was rented, I don't think we ever returned it to the store.) Here was this abrupt ending, which could not be changed. In our childish way, we adapted. We grew to regard the first few bars of "Climb Every Mountain" as the real ending. Every time we slotted in the video to watch the film, we knew that it was a journey to that song, those few opening notes, that unresolved chord. For years we carried this inside us: *The Sound of Music* ends with the nun singing.

Why did our copy of the film not have the last act? Did someone censor it? Was it just an accident? A mix-up in the recording? And why didn't we, even as children, sense that Mother Abbess had more to say, was yet to reach the climax of her performance? Looking at that fully restored scene now, Mother Abbess sings so hard she almost blows a gasket. What a cruel fate to have been cut off so unceremoniously. It was only years later, when another copy of the movie made its way into our house, that we saw, with horror, the ending.

Nothing has terrified me more.

A world of jejune frivolity was transformed into one menaced by sadistic totalitarianism and genocide. Although the film has a happy ending, with the family climbing triumphantly over the mountains into the freedom of Switzerland, the sharp disjunction between their life of comfort and one in which all are rendered fugitives hiding behind gravestones was shocking for us. So, too, was the sudden sense of physical peril when the brutalities of the natural environment had to be surmounted. There was the awful feeling of helplessness, heightened by the claustrophobia of being in the constant, blinding spotlight of celebrity, the revelation that persons who were previously lovers could now be mortal enemies. These discoveries were too much. Here was a world that was revealed to be just as fragile and changeable as the world of the Nguyamyams.

Something else was broken.

If before I could imagine myself as Maria in love, singing on the mountaintops, now I could imagine my young gay self thrown into a ghetto, forced to wear a pink triangle, policed by the state, stripped of dignity in a manner too cruel to contemplate. In her campness, in her chaffing against Catholicism, in her determination to be whoever she wanted to be, Maria became a cipher that helped me intuit both the joys and the dangers of being different. If hers was a story in which she did, eventually, climb the mountain, there was now for me a strange, refracted sense that the uphill journey of growing up gay in 1980s Trinidad was just beginning. I thought: Maria had to flee her own country to be happy, so what about me?

A single photograph can define historic moments. The man in front of four tanks in Tiananmen Square; the napalmed crying girl running towards the camera in Vietnam; the planting of a US flag on Iwo Jima; the drowned Syrian boy washed ashore. For me, the most unforgettable image from the darkest moment in Trinidad and Tobago's history was not the photograph of the police headquarters on fire after being attacked by armed insurgents; it was not the one of the leader of the attackers surrendering, dressed in all-white, his arms raised; it was not the disturbing footage, taken in parliament, of the moment when masked men stormed the chamber, taking the elected prime minister and his government hostage; it was not the broadcast in which the attackers, who had also taken over the country's lone television station, announced their insurrection. The most unforgettable image was a cartoon, *The Little Mermaid*. I was seven years old.

That Friday began like any other day. But by late afternoon, there was something strange about the sky. Where we lived, on a hill in Belmont, we could see the city right up to the Queen's Park Savannah. Some apartment towers to the west blocked our view of downtown. The sky seemed unusually cloudy, the clouds a darker grey than the fluffy white mushrooms you would ordinarily see in the afternoons. Like the people trapped in Plato's cave who saw shadows but not fire, I mistook smoke, rising in columns whipped by the wind, for rainclouds. Smoke, first from the police headquarters, then from of all the stores looted and all the offices set afire. Smoke, mistaken for something else in a world that, unknown to me, was being torn asunder.

We must have received a phone call, or heard it on the radio, or been told by a neighbour that something was wrong. By 7 pm it was clear what. The insurrectionists took to the air, claiming the country had been taken over. Except for their strange live broadcasts, all normal programming was suspended on the lone national television station, TTT. Soon, all that was showing, on perpetual loop, was *The Little Mermaid*.

Why was *The Little Mermaid* broadcast in this way? How had this film come to be selected? Did it reflect the insurgents' philosophy? Did the insurrectionists have sympathy with Ariel's search for a different life? Or was this film meant to placate, make the population docile? However it came to be, *The Little Mermaid* was both an escape from reality and a bizarre perversion of it. Its calypso-inspired songs complicated things. Like distorting mirrors, they confused as much as they fascinated. Unlike *The Sound of Music*, this was a film that was, in its own terms, not mysterious, neither in any way abridged nor incomplete. Like *Nguyamyam*, it presented a cartoon world ruled by certainties. But its mysterious provenance, the surreal circumstances of how it came to be broadcast, the fact that normally such a film would be something seen in cinemas and not broadcast freely on TV – all made it hallucinogenic.

Whoever was programming the playlist for 1990 appeared to want to cater for all demographics. *The Little Mermaid* was for children. A film for adults also played on loop during the crisis. I don't remember being particularly enthralled by *The Good, The Bad and The Ugly*. I wasn't interested in Westerns or guns. And while I was definitely interested in cowboys, the three-hour plus running time of the movie was too much. As with *The Little Mermaid*, it was hard to tell if the film somehow chimed with the agenda of the attackers. Were its gun-slinging, amoral males meant to serve as role models? Or was it chosen simply because of its long running time? Whatever the case, *The Good, The Bad and The Ugly* could not compete with *The Little Mermaid*. The mermaid music mesmerised me. For a good few weeks I danced around the yard humming Ariel's theme, believing it had magical properties. Once as

I pranced and sang, the rain started to pour. Instead of thinking my singing had provoked the rainfall, I was convinced that the melody was a powerful spell. These were days of magic. I spent the days of the coup pretending to be a grounded mermaid with the power to control the heavens.

This was a fantasy I had to honour imaginatively while carefully concealing it from everyone else. Any sign of femininity in a boy was then, as it is now, harshly policed by Trinidadian parents, aunties, siblings, friends, even complete strangers. Here was my first guilty secret, hidden in the strange limbo where cinema and reality rub against each other in powerful alchemy.

Though we are a small island society surrounded by water, and though people regularly went to the beach, deep-sea diving wasn't something many did. So the undersea world of *The Little Mermaid* still had a feeling of being alien. Its oddness matched the strange scenes unfolding around us: skies that became charcoal, army tanks patrolling the streets, men and women carrying looted items up the hills. I have a memory of seeing a man with a chandelier and wondering where he was going to put it. One group of people carried a refrigerator. The crawling army tanks, too, had an aura of the surreal. They were noisy, giant turtles.

But there was nothing out of place about Ariel's conflict. In the film, hers is a position of high privilege, yes, but also of great expectations placed on her. From the moment she fails to turn up to the musical production being put on to introduce her to society, she refuses to play the part set for her. There's a moment when she's puzzled by the world she's in. She looks at a fork, a relic from another world, and cannot fathom its use. Long after the events of July 1990 had come to their close, leaving behind an eternal wound in our society, the scene of Ariel plucking sea flower petals, like Giselle speculating whether the Prince loves her or loves her not, has stayed with me. And, yes, years later I found myself doing the same thing, but with a wrinkly hibiscus instead of seaweed or a daisy.

In the decades since 1990, books have been written, lawsuits argued, insurance claims filed, a commission of inquiry convened. And still the event maintains its horror and mystery. Years later I searched Sir David Simmons's 1,590-page report, looking for an explanation of how *The Little Mermaid* came to be on TV. There was none. Undoubtedly, the commissioners had more weighty matters to unravel. But the fact that one of the single most defining parts of the experience, a part that must have lingered in the unofficial archives in the minds of many Trinidadians, did not even feature, was a reminder of how fragile truth is. In the report, none of the main questions I had as an adult about the coup were satisfactorily addressed. How did it happen? How *could* it have happened? Was a political conspiracy involved? At the inquiry, witnesses did not testify. Documents were withheld. Court injunctions were filed and dispensed with. Decades have passed, and with it all semblance of truth. In the end, the propensity for the coup to conjure up conspiracy theories and movie-plot stories remains. In 2019, one newspaper's front-page headline was belatedly: "CIA help for T&T with coup". How the law enforcement agencies, wherever they got their help, could have allowed a sitting prime minister to be held hostage in the country's parliament building, of all places, has never been satisfactorily explained.

The coup has shown that just as we look at films over and over again without fully seeing them, so too is it hard for societies to come to terms with history. Our inability to see what is in plain sight is the manifestation of the same social forces that tell us shadows are monsters and monsters shadows. As a child, 1990 became, horrifically, a taste of a world in which what was most sacred – law, order, safety, democracy, stability – could all be thrown out of the window on a balmy Friday afternoon. As Maria had discovered, no place was safe.

Perhaps it is because we sometimes feel trapped in a never-ending bad movie that we need the cinema to escape. But the escape, no matter how dressed up, is always a return to whatever is masked or denied. In a way, all the films that have ever mattered to me have shown that what is concealed is always revealed, what is most hidden is often in plain sight.

The great film critic Roger Ebert was drawn to the movie *Wonder Boys* because it reminded him of his university days. I was drawn to the Merchant Ivory film *Maurice*, long before I knew why.

How I first came to see *Maurice* seems an unlikely story. One evening my mother was shelling pigeon peas and watching TTT, the television station that had, years prior, been taken over by the insurgents. By this stage there was no longer just one station; several had sprung up and cable was now a thing. Suddenly, you had choice. My mother could well have been watching something else on some other station that night. Maybe it was a kind of lassitude that made her leave the channel unchanged from when she had watched *The Young and the Restless*.

Maybe it was fate.

The film started. Its opening credits played over a background that looked like the brown marble from inside an old notebook. Something about it felt male and compelling, even if you did not know what lay ahead. Based on E.M. Forster's novel, *Maurice* follows two gay lovers struggling to live in Victorian England. Why it was broadcast, given its subject matter, baffles me. One would have expected the story to be too taboo for the time. By any standards, Trinidad, despite its bacchanalian Carnival pretensions, is a deeply conservative society. I sometimes wonder if the opening of the film made the broadcasters select it, unaware of its themes. Like Forster's book, the film starts on a beach. It is a school expedition. Boys and girls are being taught lessons about the sea and nature. There is kite-flying. There is tag-playing. One boy, who has no male figures in his life and is about to leave school, is given a special send-off by a paternal teacher who takes him aside and makes an awkward speech about the birds and the bees. Sex between man and woman, the teacher informs young Maurice, is "God's wondrous purpose." It might be that the broadcasters empathised with this point of view. Maybe they were satisfied with the fact that the major characters in the film, including Maurice's first lover Clive, played by Hugh Grant, fight their sexuality. Famously, Forster wanted to write a gay novel with a happy ending, but he didn't, and I've always found the book, and the faithful film adaptation, sad. Instead of ending up with the man he was meant to be with – his first love from university days – Maurice ends up far from home (like Inggolok), with the gamekeeper Scudder. The issue is not class. The issue is that although Maurice ends up with someone with whom he can be himself, Clive chooses a life of lies. You could say that if both men had lived in a different world they would have ended up where they should. Or you could say that if the Hugh Grant character had the courage to admit his true nature, they could have both been happy. Instead, when he shuts a window in the final scene, he's shutting out a life in which he could be happy, closing down his true self. If you've really invested in the film, the final chords of the score will tear you open, make you contemplate your most secret loss, rip apart every bandage you've applied in the intervening years, leave you falling to your knees, your body crossed, lame, and wanting.

All of this went over my head the first time.

Though sensing I was different, I lacked the vocabulary to articulate that difference. Life in those days worked as a kind of rehearsal space – a Felliniesque movie set. You weren't yet sure where the camera was, who your character was, or what the story was going to be. I was treading water in the way gay boys tread water before that day when, finally, they summon up the courage to tell themselves, yes, yes, *the rumours are true*.

Years later, I found *Maurice* at university and the power of art to transform life became clear. In a way, the film's wide open beach, its two men holding hands while lying in the grass, its angelic voices singing Psalm 51, its pouring rain in the cold moonlit night, its dark, musty boathouse where, quietly, someone lay in wait, hopeful: all became more real than anything that had ever happened to me on the hot streets of Port of Spain. I seized upon *Maurice*. I watched it repeatedly, obsessively. I used it as a cautionary tale or warning. I used it as a prayer. I hoped that, despite the dangers of intolerance around me, it could somehow change my world, like Ariel's singing, like Maria's climbing, like Inggolok's planet-hopping.

In this way, it already has.

ROMANTICS IN PORT OF SPAIN

Not calypso. Not soca. Not reggae. Not rapso. Not chutney. Not tassa. Not parang. Not even the steelpan music this island conjured from abandoned oil drums. No, whenever the rain falls I hear Schumann.

And by Schumann I mean one thing in particular, one piece: "Im wunderschönen Monat Mai". It's a song for piano. It's like a brief shower, less than two minutes long. The lyrics, by Heine, are in German, a language I don't speak. And yet whenever I hear it, I understand everything:

Im wunderschönen Monat Mai,
Als alle Knospen sprangen,
Da ist in meinem Herzen
Die Liebe aufgegangen.

Im wunderschönen Monat Mai,
Als alle Vögel sangen,
Da hab ich ihr gestanden
Mein Sehnen und Verlangen.

I understand everything. I go back to the first time I heard it, playing from a cassette tape in my childhood bedroom as the sun set over the ramshackle, polyglot streets of Port of Spain.

The tape was something I found on a ship. The ship had sailed into the harbour to sell books. It was a Christian missionary ship. One that sailed from shore to shore offering cheap books. The idea was to reel you in with the prospect of a bargain. Then foist bibles on you.

My sister and I didn't care for the bibles, we found the novels. And the children's books. And the comic-strips. And then, there it was on a table reserved for textbooks: a large hardcover with a picture of a violin. *Music: An Appreciation* by Roger Kamien, tape included.

That's how Robert Schumann entered the bedroom of a pubescent teenager in Trinidad on the eve of the twenty-first century. And Schubert ("Gretchen am spinnrade"). And Monteverdi ("Tu se' morta" from *L'Orfeo*). And Purcell ("Dido's Lament" from *Dido and Aeneas*). And Wagner (the prelude to Act One of *Tristan und Isolde*). And Chopin (the preludes, all twenty-four of them, including my favourite, No. 4 in E-minor).

I say that's how this music came to me. In truth, it could have come just as easily in school, in a concert hall in the city, or on the local television station (these were the days before the internet). I first heard Debussy on TV. A local celebrity host named Auntie Hazel had a children's talent show. One day a ballerina came on. She won. She had danced to "Clair de lune".

At the time, I was in the choir. To understand the implications of this, you have to understand that I was in the choir of an all-male, Roman Catholic secondary school in the heart of Port of Spain. We'd have choir practice in the music room, which was located somewhere between the school chapel and nearby Frederick Street, a street where Carnival bands would parade every year in the two days of bacchanalian revelry before Ash Wednesday.

One day, Fr Dick, our unfortunately-named principal, came to choir practice. He told us we were doing a good job, but needed to pump up the energy. He pointed at me and said, "You should be more like him as he sings, the joy on his face shines through." The boys suppressed their laughter.

It was only years later that I realised everyone in the choir was gay. (I say everyone but I really mean some of us; there *are* straight boys who like music and aren't gay after all and we should stand up for them!)

Yet, while everyone knew I was gay, I hadn't received the memo. I didn't get any action. Like a good Catholic, I remained a virgin. Which is not hard to understand if you could see what I looked like then, or if you examined my "poetry" from that period, or read the melancholy stories I wrote, or listened to the sad, sad music I imbibed.

It wasn't just the Romantics, it was Sarah McLachlan (if you don't know who that is, Wikipedia describes her as "a Canadian singer-songwriter known for her emotional ballads"), it was Bush (not Kate or even George W. but rather "an English rock band formed in London, England in 1992 known for their album *Razorblade Suitcase*"), it was Sting (when he made depressing albums like *The Soul Cages*) and the "grunge" movement of the 90s.

One good thing came from being in the choir, though. I got to hear Mr Cumberbatch sing.

Mr Cumberbatch (Eddie) was a mild-mannered mathematics teacher, who just so happened to be a first-class tenor. He went on to perform all over the world. One recess I was in the music room (where I would go to hide from the other boys) and heard him practicing. It was an arrangement, by Roger Quilter, of a poem by Shelley:

> Music, when soft voices die,
> Vibrates in the memory –
> Odours, when sweet violets sicken,
> Live within the sense they quicken.

Rose leaves, when the rose is dead,
Are heaped for the belovèd's bed;
And so thy thoughts, when thou art gone,
Love itself shall slumber on.

When he hit the word love, it was as though I was left sitting on Earth while he had launched himself to the sun. A heat came over my body. I was falling, falling, falling. *L o v e.*

After that, I went to every concert Mr Cumberbatch was in. When he sang with The Lydians choir, I was there. When he performed with my secondary school music teacher Ms Bodden-Ritch, I was there. And, years later, when he performed Schubert's song cycle *Winterreise* at the Little Carib Theatre, I was there. By that stage, I had my first boyfriend at last. He was a music connoisseur.

Though I was always around choirs, I have no real talent for singing. But it wasn't always like that.

Years before, in primary school, before my voice broke, I had been a soloist in the Music Festival put on every two years for students. The test piece was by a British composer, Peter Jenkyns. It was called "The Crocodile":

If you were to stand on the banks of the Nile
In the sweltering Sun and with sand in the air,
You'd have to beware of the bold crocodile,
For he and his friends would surely be there.

The Music Festival, in those days, was a big thing. It took place at Queen's Hall. People were fiercely competitive. Picture the world before social media, when children didn't have posts to like, videos to watch, podcasts to listen to. In this world, life becomes something like an episode of *Glee* or the film *Pitch Perfect*.

The festival was held at Queen's Hall, but the preliminary round was in the Boys Scouts Headquarters next door. The room was small and stuffy, the piano a little wonky. My primary school music teacher, Ms Merkel, played, but played too loud. In order to be heard, I had to sing as loud as I could. I belted out "The Crocodile" as though my life depended on it.

I placed first. The judges marvelled at the power of my voice. Other boys with more restraint gave me side-eye.

The semi-finals were a few weeks later at Queen's Hall, a huge auditorium with no microphones. "You have to project," Ms Merkel said.

When it was my time to sing, I was nervous. In the middle of the performance my voice cracked. I think puberty decided, then and there, to hit me with everything it had. Notes I could have previously reached were no longer within reach. My wings were clipped.

With a lashing and thrashing of terrible tail,
And a snapping and clapping of horrible jaws,
He searches for food and should he find your trail,
He wouldn't say no to a body like yours.

As I sang, the judge got up and went to the bathroom. A substitute judge took over. I later found out that the first judge had pencilled in a score of 80, the second judge erased this score, downgraded it to 76. "What happened?" Ms Merkel asked, annoyed. "Never mind. I'll let you know if you make the finals." I prayed and prayed that she would call me and give me the good news.

She never did.

One day, however, as the finals approached, something nagged me. Perhaps I already had a tendency to romanticise my life, felt I was somehow destined for a better ending. I called Queen's Hall and asked for the results. A lady on the other end of the line said my name was on the list for the finals. And the finals were happening the next night. I was lucky! All that I had needed was a score that was high enough. And I got it. God *does* work miracles!

I got my dad to drop me off at Queen's Hall the next evening (I didn't want my family to come – family makes me even more nervous). I didn't have a number for Ms Merkle but believed she'd be there. Backstage was dark, everybody was tense. I took deep breaths, and waited for my category. Every round of applause beyond the curtains vibrated in my chest. I couldn't find Ms Merkle anywhere.

"Can I help you?" a lady asked.

"Yes, I'm here for the boy's solo."

"What's your name?" I gave her my name. She checked the list. Checked again. She went over to another lady. That lady looked at her list. That lady called someone on the phone and asked them to check their list. I wasn't on it. I wasn't on any list, anywhere.

"I'm sorry, whoever said you made the finals made a mistake. We've been very busy."

★

Everyone knew I was gay before I did. One aunt called me "troubled", advised that I lose weight by chewing my food more slowly, and cautioned my parents against letting me take art lessons (her son had had a "bad experience" with an art teacher in Port of Spain, she said). It was much later that I came to realise that all the criticisms and the constant attempts at re-fashioning me were really attempts to refashion herself and her own life. And I only came to realise/admit/accept the fact of my own queerness when, in my last years of secondary school, I read *Jane Eyre*.

It might seem hard to credit this, but I pictured myself as Jane, wandering the moors, standing up to rich people, standing up to bigots, defending persecuted Helens, rejecting conventions, acting for her man, for Love. The book's Gothicism was re-mixed in my imagination, absorbed into my tropical terrain. The moors of Yorkshire became the Caroni Swamp. The blue ignis fatuus glow hanging over the marsh became the flaming *soucouyants* of local folklore who sucked your blood at night. The Gytrash was a giant, mutant pothound from the streets of St James. The fairies and sprites in Rochester's imagination became people, real people in my life. Jane took over, and I walked with her to flame. (I hadn't yet come to appreciate how her narrative had wronged Mrs Rochester, as Jean Rhys shows us.)

I became rebellious. Every month the top students would have to parade at assembly and receive special assessments cards. I crumpled mine, said to the new principal, who had replaced Fr Dick, "Education is a farce!" I shaved my curly hair. I lost weight. The new principal called me in one day, concerned.

"What's going on?" he asked.

"I wanted to get back to my roots," I said, half-jokingly, half-defiantly. He put the cigarette he was smoking into an ash tray, looked at me wearily and said, "I expected better from you." He dismissed me.

Behind the scenes, when I was not being an activist against the hegemony of the capitalist education system, I pined after a boy, wrote poems for him, made a chapbook and gave it to him. He didn't quite feel the same way. Which, after a while, became a distressingly embarrassing situation to be in.

Anybody who thinks the icy Romanticism of early 19th century music, literature and art is at odds with a tropical landscape has obviously not experienced my life.

Nor have they experienced the rain here, how it can come on suddenly like a love affair, intense, announcing itself only seconds before with lightning and thunder, the bellow of wind, of wind through trees, of deluge assailing distant surfaces, hammering, hammering galvanized roofs, a hail of metal on metal, the earth yielding its faint incense, until the frenzy is over as abruptly as it had begun, leaving nothing but the torn cerement of the sky as you wonder, *Did that just happen?*

And they obviously have not read *Jane Eyre* and its prequel *Wide Sargasso Sea*. The same deep melancholy, the same sense of wonder, of limitless imagination, the same urge to fight constraints – all can happen here, even amidst the hot bustle of our cities, even amidst the dense and colourful foliage, the pink and yellow confetti of poui trees in the hills.

★

In 2006, I was in Germany. It was the World Cup, I was visiting a friend. I was a student in Europe, in the days when being a foreign student in Europe wasn't such a scary thing. In those days, as I walked the streets of Berlin, I could tell people that I was from Trinidad, and they'd exclaim, "Ahh, the Soca Warriors!" They were referring to the fact that Trinidad and Tobago was the smallest country to ever qualify for the World Cup, had earned the moniker "Soca Warriors", named after soca, that fast-paced spinoff from calypso.

In that year, the Soca Warriors didn't get far. We lost to England (2-0). We lost to Paraguay (2-0). When we tied with Sweden (0-0), there was celebration among Trinis all over the world. We hadn't scored a single goal. But that didn't matter. At least we didn't lose yet another one.

One night over dinner, my German friend and her family started to talk about music. I couldn't speak German, but I managed to make out a reference to Schubert and "the merry month of May".

"Are you talking about "Im wunderschönen Monat Mai'?" I asked, pronouncing it perfectly. Too perfectly. My friend looked at me astonished.

"How do you know of this?"

And it was only then that it struck me how for some people it might seem odd that I, a person from the Caribbean, was a disciple of Schumann.

I, from a place where there was supposed to be nothing but sun, sand, and sea; a place where people are expected to break out in limbo-dancing spontaneously; where only short sleeves, short trousers and resort wear are worn because of the heat; where banana trees line the streets; where people all speak in a Jamaican accent; and everybody looks the same. There are no East Indians, no Chinese, no Whites, no Indigenous Peoples, no mixed people like me with my black father and East Indian mother – descendants of, respectively, slaves and indentured labourers.

And yet, despite these expectations, it was through *Jane Eyre* that I first travelled to England, and it was through "Im wunderschönen Monat Mai" that I first travelled to Germany, years before I actually set foot in these countries.

Isn't that the same country?

SOCA

Trinidadians made music from oil; and from slavery and indentureship they made soca.

Soca music evolved as the country evolved. The relationship has been complicated. Born out of the complex meeting of African and Indian traditions, calypso and the rhythms of Indian Trinidadian music, soca eventually, and tragically, became simplistic and crass. The feel-good factor of the 1980s was dropped in the 1990s, replaced with a relentless march of aerobic music, energy without charm. "Power" soca was born, its label one of the great perversions of post-colonial history. It echoed the rhetoric of the 1970's Black Power movement, but jettisoned the ideals of an egalitarian society in favour of a return to the brutal whip of the hedonistic imperatives: Jump! Wave! Misbehave!

By the 2000s, concessions had to be made to an altered environment in which music was now part of a different global matrix of production and distribution. As Carnival costumes became skimpier – yet more and more expensive – the art form took on higher production values to add an air of legitimacy to what had reverted, in another perversion of history, into a bourgeois street parade. The innovations, however, did not mask the bastardisation of soca's status, its pigeon-holing as a once-a-year-phenomenon, its status as the less cool sibling of dub, reggae, hip-hop, R&B and soul.

By the 2010s, the power explosion cooled. Jump! Wave! Misbehave! had exhausted the genre to the point of death. Costumes, shorn of all fabric, had nowhere left to go. In the ennui, reversals became inevitable. To break the listlessness, mas took back fabric. The Lost Tribe was found. "Groovy" soca, a slow, more melodious version, became the new norm. It rose to the top by virtue of being the only version of soca left standing. For a moment, soca acknowledged that music could be emotional, could have feeling, could be human, as though the women and men who had been treated as chattels for past centuries were finally being given permission to breathe. Lost in time, groovy soca, in its highest form, is the echoing sigh of the slave and indentured labourer.

But by 2019, when Kees Dieffenthaller, a soca star whose band shares the name of the famous Ken Loach film about a boy and his falcon, was singing "Savannah Grass", there was a resurgence of jump, wave, misbehave.

"Power is back", declared the chairman of the International Soca Monarch, Fay Ann Lyons-Alvarez. Lyons-Alvarez should know a thing or two about power. Her father, Austin "Superblue" Lyons, had been power soca's principle exponent, winning the road march several times. Her husband, Ian "Bunji Garlin" Alvarez, a soca artist with an experimental edge, was in the running for that year's road march with a song called "Famalay".

To understand the confusing tug of forces at work in 2019, it is instructive to look at the road march race between "Savannah Grass", performed by Dieffenthaller, and "Famalay", performed by Skinny Fabulous, Machel Montano and Bunji Garlin.

"Savannah Grass" is an unabashed poem to the land, the Queen's Park Savannah. As Walt Whitman found grass to be "a uniform hieroglyphic", Dieffenthaller's song sees the savannah, the ultimate destination for all Carnival bands – the large stage on which masqueraders show off their costumes – as a great leveller, a stage for all the contradictions of life, where divisions are mended, opposites reconciled. "Is the place of bacchanal", Dieffenthaller declares. "In this sweet botanical, this Carnival". The word botanical alludes not only to what is natural but also to a specific place – the Botanical Gardens that adjoins the Savannah, a popular destination for families and for wedding parties taking photographs. The Savannah destination becomes both a stage and an altar to love, a carnival within the carnival in which each individual has their own journey to make but must, in the end, yield to the ultimate forces: love and death. The old, banal imperatives are thus clothed in new meaning:

> I want you to find your way
> Everybody on stage
> Oh Lord oh
> If you coming down from the mountains
> Oh God oh
> When the rhythm beating in town
> See we jumping on
> The Savannah Grass, the Savannah Grass
> You could see it all when the dust raise
> Oh Lord oh
> When the people tell yuh they cannot wait
> Oh God oh
> Feel the spirit jumping in town
> We coming round
> The Savannah Grass, the Savannah Grass

Dieffenthaller's dulcet tones transmit the same meaning as the lyrics. "Is love we feeling," he sings. "Look everybody revelling." An overlay of dissonant textures lends forward propulsion: a journey to a resolution. The soca's opening is also its ending: "If you know, yeah / Then you know, yeah." The sense is of something intuited, of a shared communal consciousness, momentarily manifested, inducted from bodies, liberated first on the streets, then on the savannah grass.

A sense of community is also ostensibly behind "Famalay". Despite the depth and exuberance implied by its title, it is an unchallenging, repetitive song, without soul, more appropriate for a spin class than a celebration of the flesh. It was an underwhelming outing for all concerned. Gone was the metaphor of Montano's previous hit, "Soca Kingdom". Gone was the emotion of Bunji Garlin's "Carnival Tabanca". Instead, a lion roars, and deep male voices celebrate being deep male voices. And yet, "Famalay" convincingly wins the Road March title, beating "Savannah Grass" by a margin of 346 plays to 207.

Race was very much a factor in all of this. Though both songs were paeans to racial unity, their singers were from different worlds and appealed to different bases. Dieffenthaller, whose family originally came from Austria, via Holland, was seen as a vestige of the veneration of lighter skin tones, the white plantation class. Montano, Garlin and Fabulous were unabashedly black.

And unabashedly male. "Famalay" reflected prevailing gender norms in which the male was rough, harsh, percussive. That depth of feeling was jettisoned was no coincidence. This was simply a reflection of the social constructs that associate the emotional with weakness, weakness with the female, the female with the inferior. The idea of Caribbean unity is a wonderful ideal. But "Famalay" as a production is co-opted by a greater call to action: a militaristic call to reassert notions of manliness. The award of the Road March to this song was a way for Trinidadians, unsure of their claims to power, to close ranks behind three men presenting a crude, backward vision of manliness. "Savannah Grass" with its sweeter, more emotional tones presented by a man had to be rejected; its singer denigrated as an "other", an aberration, a scar, an all-too-complex reminder of our diversity.

SNAKES AND LADDERS

In the days when children played board games, everyone in Trinidad played Snakes and Ladders. Those were simple times, and it was a simple game. You raced along a grid of squares towards a finish line. With the roll of the dice, you might end up on a snake and would have to slide down, back along the path from which you had progressed. Or you might end up on a ladder, and get to climb up, inching closer to heaven. The game was everywhere: in stores on Charlotte Street or in the big malls to the west. For many of us it seemed part and parcel of growing up. And for a long time, the snakes on the version we had at home in Belmont were the only snakes I ever saw.

Belmont was a place where it was relatively hard to encounter wild animals. There might be a stray iguana every now and then, maybe an agouti, a few birds. Although we were walled in by verdant hills to the north, the narrow lanes, densely packed concrete houses and busy streets had more of an urban feel. Not like nearby places like Cascade, where the line between suburb and jungle could suddenly evaporate. Or parts of Morvant where you could think you were in the country and had gone back in time. Maybe other children, perhaps along the Belmont Valley Road or up Belle Eau Road, had better luck finding reptiles. But for the most part, I felt lucky if I found a lizard in our concrete yard. Snakes were limited to the fat, dangling things on the board game, made ever more memorable because they had black and white stripes, as though they were in prison.

It was years later that I discovered where Snakes and Ladders came from, that it was an ancient Indian game called *Moksha Patam*, that some say the Marathi poet-saint Gyandev created it in the 13th century, that it was meant to be a morality lesson, that the original game had one-hundred squares, the 12th square was faith, the 51st square reliability, the 57th square generosity, the 76th square knowledge, and the 78th square asceticism. These were the ladders. The snakes were the 41st square for disobedience, the 44th square for arrogance, the 49th square for vulgarity, the 52nd square theft, the 58th square lying, the 62nd square drunkenness, the 69th square debt, the 73rd square murder, the 84th square anger, the 92nd square greed, the 95th square pride, and the 99th square lust. The 100th square was Nirvana.

How Snakes and Ladders came to Trinidad is a fascinating question. Did

East Indian labourers bring the game during the time of colonial indentureship? Or did it come in a more roundabout way, first being transported to England from India, then returning via the colonial power to British Trinidad? Or did it come from America, having been introduced there in 1943 under the name Chutes and Ladders?

I can still see the green squares of the version we played, unconscious of the long, complex history that brought it to our house, the thinking that lay just beneath its surface, its message of the balance between karma and kama, destiny and desire, and the strange certainty that the game presents us with a Markov chain – from any square on the board the odds of moving to another square are fixed and independent of any previous game history, absorbing all the movements in a dance to one end.

"That which is pure consciousness itself, without the quality of being conscious, is not conscious of itself," Gyandev wrote. "Can the eyeball perceive itself? Can the sky enter into itself? Can the fire burn itself?" If a long, complicated history brought Snakes and Ladders to my trough, then pure luck brought me D.H. Lawrence's poem "Snake".

It was a rainy day in Port of Spain and I was at the school May fair. I was at an all-boys Catholic secondary school. The May fair was the annual fund-raising event. The cool boys looked forward to the disco at which reggae, dub, and hip-hop would reportedly be played, while the rest of us had to be content with food stalls, a book sale, and a lucky dip. I dipped my hand into the bran tub, which was an empty oil drum filled with wood shavings, and pulled out something disappointing, like a soft drink or an item of tinned food. Among the books at the book sale I saw *A Choice of Poets*. I liked its blue spine, its cover. A woman stood next to a bridge, staring thoughtfully at a river, as though she had come to the May fair and was bored. For a long time I liked the idea of possessing this book more than the book itself. The cleanness of the font on the cover, the brightness of the blue spine, the weight of its smooth paper.

In those days I liked building things and rearranging the furniture in my room. I had just installed a new desk, made with concrete bricks and some leftover planks of wood from one of my father's handyman projects. I realised I needed something to read on this new desk. Luckily, I had just the thing. I opened *A Choice of Poets*, and came upon the poem:

A snake came to my water-trough
On a hot, hot day, and I in pyjamas for the heat,
To drink there.

Here's the thing. This poem is one of the most anthologized in the world. School children everywhere are made to read it. But as a boy growing up in Belmont it felt shocking. I had a reaction I was sure no one else could have. For the first time I saw language bend to its subject matter. Something pulsed. The arrangement of the words, their sounds and ideas, the conflict of the narrator, the fragmented free verse that still seemed to fall into place, like pieces of broken pottery being slowly reassembled.

The first line runs on to the second, as though in prelude to some action about to be taken, some event. The conjunction "and" followed by the subject "I" makes us think a verb will follow, such as, "and I screamed" or "and I looked". But then, a defiance in the line sets in. The narrator is now "in pyjamas", wrapped, swaddled, passive. An explanation is given for the garb; it's "for the heat". Here, we are accustomed to heat, so the idea of dressing for it seemed oddly ritualistic. At this stage, a verb is still possible after this digression, such as "and I in pyjamas for the heat, / ran away". But when the verb comes, it applies to the snake, not the pyjama-wearing narrator. Or does it?

It's a stunning elision that asks us to question the difference between animal and man, between states of knowledge or self-consciousness, between good and bad, chastity and lust. In the next stanza, this merger of the snake with the "I" continues.

> In the deep, strange-scented shade of the great dark carob tree
> I came down the steps with my pitcher
> And must wait, must stand and wait, for there he was at the trough before me.

The assignment of a gender to the snake raises questions of sexuality. The carob tree is notable for its phallic pods. There is a sensual description of the snake drinking, before Lawrence declares:

> Someone was before me at my water-trough,
> And I, like a second-comer, waiting.

It feels explosive. The encounter with the snake makes the narrator come into being. The mirror image forces a confrontation with the self. A kind of rationality is given to the snake, who drinks and lifts his head "as cattle do", yet he seems an elemental being, wrought from the "burning bowels of the earth". Hell is implied, but at the same time Lawrence grounds things in a geographic reality. The events are happening, "On the day of Sicilian July, with Etna smoking." The snake, thus, is both a mystical creature and the inorganic expression of bigger forces.

The sexual symbolism of the snake, who returns to "the earth-lipped fissure in the wall-front" is clear. As is the poem's questioning of the place of human beings in the animal kingdom. As is its examination of the interplay between temptation and taboo, right and wrong, the free and the imprisoned. Less noticeable is the poem's subtle argument for its own sinuosity, for the slowing down of time through language, for mantras that echo and question volition, cause, and effect.

Snakes and Ladders is a game that teaches you binaries. You land on a snake, you go down. You land on a ladder, you go up. There are only two options and it all depends on fate. But D.H. Lawrence's "Snake" blurs the forked path that Robert Frost sets in front of us. Choice and fate confront the narrator. But his ambivalence, his passive aggressiveness, his simultaneous attraction and repulsion, places him between action against the snake and surrender to the animal, and what the animal represents: secret self. That he comes to strike the animal is a moment of parapraxis, an accident revealing the currents within him. Discovering this poem was discovering in art, and in the simple arrangement of words and facts, a new game entirely.

DYLAN THOMAS: THREE ENCOUNTERS
(WITH APOLOGIES TO MARGARET ATWOOD)

In 2014, shortly after I turned thirty, I wrote an essay about Dylan Thomas. The essay followed a journey I made with my aunt, Ann Marie, to find the poet's grave in Laugharne, the town in Wales where he is buried. The essay of about 2,000 words was written in the form of diary entries.

But there were gaps.

Some days were omitted, a stylistic device used, perhaps, to build mystery. I didn't mention my aunt. I didn't mention flying from Trinidad to London via St Lucia, as the local airline did in those days, then taking a train from London to Wales, then taking another train and taxi to Laugharne. I must have been very dedicated to Thomas, which, as I recall, I was. But why? I'm wondering this as I re-read my essay now. As so often when folks attempt to tackle Dylan Thomas – or any writer whose work everyone knows yet no one knows – my real subject was not the author of the poems but the author of the essay, me. "When someone starts telling me about the truth," observes the psychiatrist in the 2007 remake of *The Invasion of the Body Snatchers*, "what I hear is what they are telling me about themselves." Amen.

I start off on a bemused note: "We are in the strangest town in Wales." Fair enough. But why I find the town strange is not clear. As I had learned from my days of writing newspaper stories, I try to suck the reader in. I hold back on any explanation until the next section of the essay in which I describe a scene in a pub. On the wall of this pub is a poster that advertises Laugharne as "the strangest town in Wales". A bartender just so happens to explain what is strange about the town. He says, "You'll understand what's strange easily. People here are really, really nice." Memory plays tricks. I might have made up the poster. Might. But I *definitely* made up the expository dialogue. Not made up, though, was what came next.

There is a bizarre story involving a white couple who had come to the pub to have a pint. This couple stares at my aunt and myself brazenly. The woman remarks, "You're both so beautiful". Though I mention this dialogue in the essay, the race of the couple is not specified, nor is the awkwardness of suddenly realising that Wales is still a place where, except for places like Butetown in Cardiff, black and brown bodies are exotic birds, rarely spotted among the flora and fauna of the marshland. Something of my unease, however, finds its way into the narrative, transformed by a focus on odd details, such as when the elderly husband tells us they are from a competing pub down the road, and discretely slips us a card, then says of his offensive yet charismatic wife, "She could get away with murder." Nowhere do I say the pub was a fitting place to write about because Thomas drank himself to death and would sometimes drink at that very pub when he was in town. I do take care to note that the bartender is the youngest person within miles, though I don't mention his fit body, his charming smile, his intriguing tattoos and piercings. Still, as with my reaction to the racism, an indication of my thirst creeps in: the section ends on a phallic note: "That night in bed, I think of the town's famous clock tower, standing black and white against the sky, just two blocks away." It's the clock tower from *Under Milk Wood* and it's the closest I get to getting laid in the essay.

Eventually, Thomas's grave appears. One paragraph is devoted to its yellow, red, and purple flowers; its simple white cross with the words, "In Memory of Dylan Thomas"; its telling detail involving Thomas's wife, Caitlin, buried in the same plot. There's a complete lack of poetry to the place – a kind of silence I was very drawn to.

The rest of the essay is devoted to making a single point. It argues that a writer's life is relevant to understanding the writing. "If we admit the landscape is in the poem, is the life not there too?" I ask. "Reading a poem is like reading a poet and, in turn, everything that has touched him. In this way, the reader and poet converge and something universal sparks between them."

It all drinks, blissfully, at the fountain of Thomas but does not betray the real reason for my devotion. It's only now, as I re-read it that it's clear to me I was obsessed with finding Thomas's grave because of my own grief over the death of someone close to me, namely the nurturing newspaper editor who had taught me a lot about writing; my desire to hero-worship someone else; and my search for some kind of god when the shocking reality of death had upended the comfortable agnosticism of my life as a lapsed Catholic. Despite the argument of the essay, I held back details in search of something universal. But it was those seemingly tiny, biographical details, the details that rubbed and boiled up beneath the surface of the page, visible like a body trapped under the frozen surface of a lake, those details were the telling points of universal significance. Here I was turning poetry into my new god, and Dylan Thomas into my new high priest, but with nothing to show for it on the surface of the writing.

However, in the essay I do provide an interesting reading of Thomas's "Poem in October". I argue it is meant to be an immersive experience, transformed when read *in situ* at the Dylan Thomas Walk that overlooks Laugharne. The walk provides a spectacular view of the Tâf estuary, which opens like a fan at low-tide, and of Thomas' famous boathouse where he sometimes wrote. From there you can see the Gower, north Devon, Caldey Island, and Tenby. "The marsh environment comes to mirror the processes not only of war, but of economy and society generally," I wrote. "Reading the poem on the page is nothing like reading the poem along the specially-designed walk which now exists. At several spots, stations have been made bearing sections of the poem relating to the landscape, as well as old, faded maps and drawings of the view. Only by taking the Dylan Thomas Walk can you fully appreciate what he meant."

Though I alluded to World War II, I didn't go into Thomas' views on war. Nor the fact that he was declared too frail, but flirted with being a conscientious objector. I also dodged the obvious point that most people cannot be required to go through all this trouble just to read one poem. I ignored the reality that all poems must eventually take on a life of their own, independent of the conditions that generated them. I paid little heed to the idea that poems are not reductive puzzles meant to be solved, for which there is one meaning or solution or interpretation, superior to all others, and that the mystery of the poem, the areas where we are unsure, is what makes poetry poetry. As Thomas himself said, "The best craftsmanship always leaves holes and gaps in the works of the poem so that something that is not in the poem can creep, crawl, flash or thunder in."

The fact that the Dylan Thomas Walk replicates an experience that bears a great resemblance to the Stations of the Cross was not something I felt necessary to devote attention too. Though I fancied myself a Dylan Thomas groupie, I had yet to discover the conflicts that divided his family. His mother was a devout Christian, his father an atheist. Maybe his preference for his mother explains why there is an evangelical sound to his poems, even when the content is irreverent. Being made to venture along the walk turns his poetry into a spiritual exercise: a kind of proselytising that is inappropriate given the lack of didacticism in his verse. At the same time, it is paradoxically fitting because his poems can feel like sermons. He co-opts the tactics of the hot gospeller.

While I was aware of the notion of psychogeography, I had yet to apply it to the strange and wild landscape at Laugharne. I did not seek to examine in what ways the rhythms of the environment, with its quick tides and unique birds, plants and trees, might have affected other poets from the area in the way it affected Thomas. It fascinates me now, though it did not fascinate me then, to think of a collective consciousness at work, writing Laugharne into a shared construct.

I could have added a whole section to my essay indicating how, had I really wanted to encounter Thomas, all I had to do was read Caribbean poets of a certain generation instead of trekking thousands of miles to visit his grave. I could have sketched the powerful influence of his style on post-colonial poets. His use of pun, portmanteau-words, paradox, allusion, paranomasia, paragram, catachresis, slang, assonantal rhymes, vowel rhymes, sprung rhythm, twistings and convolutions – all turn up like flotsam in the sea of West Indian poetry. I could have pointed to Derek Walcott's "A City's Death By Fire", whose title, and not the title alone, echoes Thomas's "A Refusal to Mourn the Death, by Fire, of a Child in London". I could have taken note of V.S. Naipaul's citing of this Walcott poem in his claim that early Walcott was stuck in an "imitative quagmire". I could have discovered how Neville Dawes transferred the hawk of "St John's Hill" to the ancestral space of Sturge Town, Jamaica in poems such as "Fugue" and "Acceptance". I could have considered how Samuel Selvon, when he came to write his stunning 1971 poem "Discovering Tropic", borrowed and re-phrased Thomas's most famous opening line: "To begin at the beginning". I could have pointed to several Caribbean writers being, at one point or another, compared to Thomas with his rich, deep tones; how Thomas and Caribbean writers gravitated to radio work at the BBC. But I missed that chance.

Nor did I make anything of the parallels between Wales and the Caribbean, how both are societies with relatively small populations, how they were at various points annexed by Britain, how a revival of Welsh nationalism appeared to coincide with the Caribbean Independence movement of the 1960s, and how the lure of Thomas's lines for Caribbean poets, may therefore have been freighted with subliminal political associations. It's just possible too that Thomas's poem "And Death shall have No Dominion" might even have inspired at least one of the black and brown soldiers from the colonies who fought in World War II as British Empire troops.

One aspect of Dylan Thomas's poetry that has drawn raging debate is the relationship between sound and sense. Pope had famously argued, "The sound must seem an Echo of the sense". According to some critics, in his later work Thomas had reversed the relationship. Derek Stanford found "a felicity to diction... covering a monotony of perception"; Elder Olson detected a "copiousness of language, his eloquence, booming at us, working on us too obviously, even exciting us unnecessarily"; while Robert Graves declared, "Dylan Thomas was drunk with melody, and what the words were he cared not." On the other hand, William T. Moynihan heard a devotion to "auditory effects", not sentimental rhetoric. And Louise Baughan Murdy, who wrote an entire book on the matter, called for "an expansive poetry in which sound supports sense and contributes to the total meaning". All of this assumes that a poem should on some level make sense, even as we are yet to agree what "sense" is. I could have suggested that Thomas's use of sound renders his poems scores, sculptures, like the diamonds and anvils of his poem "Vision and Prayer" that seem to pay homage to George Herbert's pattern poems. And as it relates to sound being dismissed as inferior to sense, I could have seen another parallel here with

West Indian writers whose work is often expected to have exotic sounds and flavours, though not much else. I could have mentioned the dismissal of Caliban as a noisy, primitive brute, despite him having the best lines in *The Tempest*. I could have noted how Thomas defined poetry as, "memorable words-in-cadence which move and excite me". And I could have suggested how both sides of the spectrum of sense and nonsense constitute poetry, whether we are dealing with a sophisticated process poem generated by a computer algorithm or a nonsense verse by Edward Lear.

Though I chose to address my relationship with Dylan Thomas in prose – in a move that seemed to make a point about the poetic potential of this kind of writing – there was no questioning of prose as my chosen medium. Nor did I examine how Thomas's own prose relates to his poetry. Both are united by an attention to sound. The synergy between the two – a synergy Thomas exploited in some of his more successful short stories such as "After the Fair" and "A Child's Christmas in Wales" – was not covered. How the latter story evokes a social milieu that bears much resemblance to aspects of Trinidadian society was not picked up. Nor were the similarities between the Welsh and the Trinidadian accents; the latter, you should know, was recently voted the eleventh sexiest accent in the world, way above the Welsh but trailing the Scottish and Irish.

Why was Thomas so important to me?

Like a difficult poem, I had amassed detail after detail, fact after fact, and yet the essence of things remained a mystery. I had aimed to show how biographical details of a poet could enhance our understanding of their work, yet, like a good reporter, I seemed hell-bent on not becoming the story. The journey with my auntie, a maternal figure in my life; the mourning for my editor who died abruptly while on the job; the hagiography of Thomas, turning him into an idolized father – I seemed in search of parents. This, even as my own parents were alive and well. What did it mean? Did it have something to do with the context of my own life as a gay person from the Caribbean, a queer person, seen and unseen, perpetually coming out to people? Perpetually seeking, yet not seeking, approval? From parental figures? Others? A surprising place to end up, I guess, after travelling to Wales.

I closed my essay with a complicating paradox. "The more we know of a poet," I argued, "the more possibilities are inherent in the text the poet leaves behind, even if the poem, like the poet, remains unknowable." Here, at least, I was on to something, even if it meant acknowledging there are things I would never know about Thomas and, by implication, myself.

ISHION HUTCHINSON

First, he writes it all out on a yellow legal pad. The language flows, pages and pages. He works on a red wooden desk made from a repurposed door. He sits daily at this desk, up early in the mornings at 6 am, watching light rise over buildings in the distance.

He's not in Jamaica any more. This is Salt Lake City, Utah, a place where there is no water, no sea. Instead, he creates an ocean for himself, right there on the page, his images cascading, taking orbital motion, swashing, breaking, foaming, releasing ideas as a wave throws up flotsam.

He writes draft after draft, fluidly, over weeks, then types it all up, prints it all out. By the tenth iteration he senses he might be a little closer. He cuts, cuts, cuts. More cuts; themes are condensed, strands taken up. Until, years after he began, he arrives at a place that matches his intuition about what this poem should be.

"I needed velocity," he said, "velocity that could be so rapid, as if it were mad brush strokes on a canvas in which the narrative is only within the strokes – the story crystallised to the point where it does not stand any more and all that is left is the speed of it."

The resulting poem tells us something about him.

"At nights birds hammered my unborn," it begins. It continues, over the course of fourteen lines that move with the velocity of water, into a stunning transformation:

> I smashed my head against a lightbulb
> and light sprinkled my hair; I rejoiced, a poui
> tree hit by the sun in the room, a man, a man.

This became the centre of *House of Lords and Commons*, a collection that conjures, through words, the turbulence, erosion, motion of the sea.

Hutchinson was in Port of Spain some time ago to take part in the inaugural Derek Walcott Festival, a series of events put on by the Walcott estate to commemorate the late Nobel laureate. He sat in the lobby of the Kapok Hotel, at one time a haunt of Walcott's, wearing a striped shirt from the Gold Coast. Just as his fashion crossed boundaries, so too has done the poet. Since starting to write in Port Antonio, Jamaica, his poetry has taken him to places such as Baltimore, New York, Rome, London, Berlin.

But his exploration of the world began closer to home.

"Trinidad was the first place I ever travelled to when I was in my first year at UWI," Hutchinson told me. "I spent a summer in Tobago. It's the surprise of poetry that I've been all over. It makes you a traveller."

Yet no matter how far the journey, he always returns to one place. "I was born in Port Antonio, in a little town of the eastern section of Jamaica in a parish called Portland."

His mother, Hermine, and father, Ira, were Rastafarians who worked in the Port Antonio market. Poetry was not a word at the forefront of life, but the spear of language was. Hermine would set exercises in Hummingbird copybooks for her children.

"She would start a story and I would pick it up. I was eight years old at the time. My mother worked a lot with making things. She would crotchet and knit."

More threads for his passion would be added when his father, Ira, moved to London.

"We wrote each other," Hutchinson said. "This kind of communication was part of my young childhood. In one letter I was trying to figure out my own ambitions and I wrote that I wanted to be a journalist. The letters were weekly, from nine years old up to sixth form." So whether in epistolary form or through discrete exercises, a feeling for narratives of becoming emerged.

Hutchinson's close relationship with his grandmother May was also pivotal.

"She was a very quiet woman, very reserved. She always liked and preferred to be by herself. I clung to her."

May was a baker, and Hutchinson went to live with her for extended periods.

"In my work there is the ghost of a place," he said. "I always seem to be writing from the same place, which is specifically the landscape I grew up in, particularly my grandmother's house, which is built on a hill in Port Antonio. This house overlooks the sea. In a sense my stirring into language was this specific place. This is the nucleus. Everything grows out of that.

"In front of this view the sea has a visual limit and seems as if something you could walk down to and arrive at. But in fact any kind of movement towards results in it moving away, becoming more distant. There is always this chase, as if I am lured to chase that image of the sea."

Hutchinson might as well be describing the effect of his own poetry. Even when ostensibly addressing subjects that do not relate to the coast, such as "Station" or "Anthropology" from his first book, *Far District*, his lines embody the ebb and flow, the multitudinous forces within the crest of a wave. Meaning and narrative are telegraphed and undermined; we surf and dive until we get a sense of the poet himself plumbing the depths, retrieving truth from the interstices of the complex play of waves.

Little wonder Hutchinson has thus far received the US National Book Critics Circle Award for Poetry, a Guggenheim Fellowship, the Whiting Writers Award, the PEN/Joyce Osterweil Award and the Larry Levis Prize from the Academy of American Poets. He was recently announced as a recipient of a Windham-Campbell Prize, alongside figures such as Kwame Dawes and David Chariandy.

All of it has allowed Hutchinson to deepen his love of language. "West Ride Out" – a poem published in the Autumn 2017 issue of *The Poetry Review* – shows a writer committing even more unequivocally to a radical embrace of prose within the framework of flowing lyricism, turning back to John Donne yet moving forward into a line that is as sensual as it is broken: "And love grows angel in the gloam," it begins, "with your calls through resistant stars." In his language, the poet seems ever nearer to transforming, at last, into seawater.

THE SHOW MUST GO ON

Keats, if he does not say it, implies it: all poets are actors. In a letter to a friend, he describes the "poetical Character" thus:

> … it is not itself – it has no self – it is everything and nothing – It has no character – it enjoys light and shade; it lives in gusto, be it foul or fair, high or low, rich or poor, mean or elevated – It has as much delight in conceiving an Iago as an Imogen. What shocks the virtuous philosopher, delights the camelion Poet... A Poet is the most unpoetical of any thing in existence; because he has no Identity – he is continually in for – and filling some other Body – The Sun, the Moon, the Sea and Men and Women who are creatures of impulse are poetical and have about them an unchangeable attribute – the poet has none.

It's hard to say just how far Keats was willing to take this. Is it a manifesto for the life of the poet, or a statement about the appropriate range of poetry's subject matter? Both? At the least, these comments encourage us to think about the similarities, if any, between performance and poetry.

If poetry is concerned with creating experiences, perhaps this is what links it to the idea of performance. Just as actors aim to provoke emotion or convey feeling and ideas through tools such as gesture and body language, so too do poets aim to evoke feeling, albeit through the artefacts of words drizzled on a page; or type carved onto objects; or text on a computer screen; or writ large on walls by high-tech projectors.

Given its fluidity and capacity for empathy, we might interpret Keats to be saying that the "poetical Character" can be understood as a kind of acting and acting a kind of poetry. At a basic level, of course, the poem may be performed, especially if it is written as a monologue or a piece for voices (such as Dylan Thomas's closet drama *Under Milk Wood* – or some of the poems in Pamela Mordecai's book *Subversive Sonnets*, discussed below). Similarly, the actor must co-opt the techniques of poetry if she is to achieve what she seeks to do with an audience. Acting is as much about what is not said as said; it is a choreography of silence, speech, gesture, implication, sound, and sight. Both poetry and acting aim to replicate human experience and feeling in some way. Both, Aristotle would probably say, spring from the same imitative instinct.

Yet, if poets are actors, are we not all actors, too? Shakespeare has many answers to this. One version is in *Macbeth*:

Life's but a walking shadow, a poor player
That struts and frets his hour upon the stage
And then is heard no more: it is a tale
Told by an idiot, full of sound and fury,
Signifying nothing.

Another, markedly different version, comes later in *The Tempest*:

Our revels now are ended. These our actors,
As I foretold you, were all spirits and
Are melted into air, into thin air:
And, like the baseless fabric of this vision,
The cloud-capp'd towers, the gorgeous palaces,
The solemn temples, the great globe itself,
Yea, all which it inherit, shall dissolve
And, like this insubstantial pageant faded,
Leave not a rack behind. We are such stuff
As dreams are made on, and our little life
Is rounded with a sleep.

A similar perception came more recently, from the novelist J.G. Ballard. At the age of fifteen Ballard left decimated Shanghai, where he'd spent the Second World War under Japanese occupation, for Cambridge. He remarked:

One of the things I took from my wartime experiences was that reality was a stage set... The comfortable day-to-day life, school, the home where one lives and all the rest of it... could be dismantled overnight.

One reason that the idea of life as a theatrical production endures is because it presents tantalising possibilities. What comes at the end of this play? If "real life" is a play, then are we not partaking of plays within plays, ad infinitum?

Aside from this, the conceit endures because it is, simply, convincing. It touches on something of the artificiality of all communication, all language; it reflects philosophical questions about cause and effect, determinism, free-will, and fate; it focuses on the idea of creation and the realm of the imagination; it reminds us how personality itself can be a roving, fungible creation.

In truth, the idea of life as a performance on a stage endures because it forces us to question what is true and what is not. A fiction can sometimes be more truthful to life than factual reality. The actor can create something freer and more alive in an audience than what exists outside the theatre. The point of the lie, then, becomes one of blurring the line and, in a strange, ventriloquistic way, telling a truth.

★

Not only do the poems in Jane King's *Performance Anxiety* (2013) suggest ways of looking at the poet as a performer, but they explore the idea of personality as a performance. The book's first section comprises new poems, while two other sections select from King's previous collections, *Fellow Traveller* (1994) and *Into the Centre* (1993).

King was born in St Lucia, where she recently retired as dean of the Division of Arts, Science, and General Studies at the Sir Arthur Lewis Community College. In addition to being an award-winning poet, she has a number of acting and directing credits, and was a founding director of the Lighthouse Theatre Company. Her newest poems do not explicitly deal with theatre. Instead, they take up an ambivalent posture and attitude to the conducting of different roles relating to social and family duties, such as mother, lover, friend, poet, dean, devotee. The idea of performance is re-enforced through evocative titles such as "The Performer's Night Terror", "The Performer's Love Poem", "Performers are Holy", and "Performer After the Tropical Storm".

In these poems, the playing of different roles is tied to existential questions raised by a range of social contexts and constructs. In the opening poem, "Same Circus, Second Year", the stage is offstage. A family has come to see a show, but who is really putting on a show in this "eerie circus light"? A son observes animals:

> Three once-white ducks are crammed into
> a cage with muddy floor
> the toddlers gravitate to them
> Mikel asks what they're for
>
> To lay the eggs to feed the snakes
> and what are the snakes for?
> To put their heads in a lady's mouth...
>
> Then what's the lady for?
>
> Oh, we're frightened, we are weary
> we are hungry, sick and sore
> and the crowd calls out for more
> always
> the crowd calls
> out
> for more

The enjambment of the last stanza makes it polyvalent. "We" are both members of the crowd and its entertainers. "We" are constantly "sick and sore" and part of that thirsting crowd, even if a comma separates us. The crowd beckons; the crowd calls all the time; the crowd demands accountability, maybe blood too – just as it expresses delight ("out for

more"); and goes in search of meaning elsewhere ("out / for more").
It is telling that this kind of kaleidoscopic breakdown of meaning in
the poem comes after the queries of the child, who asks the simple
yet difficult questions the adults are struggling to answer. A routine
scene in which a curious child's probing questions grow tiresome to
exhausted parents becomes freighted with existential concerns.

"What's the lady for?" may well refer to a general question about the
place of the female in this show, as well as wider questions asked by the
feminist school. Earlier at the start of the poem, a "dancing girl" is
objectified, falls, and is "caught by hired local men in tired velvet clothes."
The poem's persona remarks: "it's not rehearsed, it isn't fun." This circus
is supposed to be an entertainment, yet it turns sour because it comes to
mirror larger forces at work. The family unit is also implicated in this, for
it is the family that comes to the show and performs the role of audience,
making it unclear who is really who, because the family in reality comprises
individuals playing specific roles within its dynamic – and for the benefit
of a crowd. So, "Same Circus" achieves a disorientating critique effortlessly, unfurling swiftly to show the innards of the stage set. It follows
Dylan Thomas's suggestion that a well-crafted poem "leaves holes and gaps
in the works of the poem so that something that is not in the poem can
creep, crawl, flash, or thunder in."

King's vision is honest and wide-ranging: encompassing the personal
and the social in economically crafted poems that are wry, disarming, and
effective. In "Performer After the Tropical Storm", the storm may well be
between two people ("I do not know how to say / all this to you") or two
countries or regions. A similar process occurs in "The Other Sea Almond
Women After the Storm". In "The Performer Gets Some Comfort from a
Tree", the stand-out poem of her book, trees themselves come to be
performers:

> A tree told me that nourishment
> is never very far from where we are,
> that it is our most delicate filaments
> that force the dust and rock aside and travel far
> to tap the water, mine the minerals we need,
> that it is our most vulnerable tips, like leaves
> so casually blown, that search the air, like seeds
> so tiny, bravely grow, whatever one believes.
>
> The tree said: Know, you must sit still and slow.
> Everything you need to grow is all around,
> it's hidden in the rocks in the hard ground,
> it's in the harsh and mocking wind. You know
> you cannot strain and fight to dig these out.
> What's softest, most vulnerable, conquers drought.

The sonnet's metaphors and images embody contradiction and complexity. In a graceful nod to Eric Roach's poem, "The Flowering Rock", the "delicate filaments" of the tree roots conquer "the hard rock". Patience, a steadfast nature, and wiliness overcome drought. One can argue that the poet's and the actor's craft gain from similar allegiances to subtlety, economy and all endeavours that involve seemingly insurmountable challenges. Other poems in the book contain apparent dichotomies that are undermined, in bravura fashion, to reveal what are in fact indissoluble, linked contraries and show unexpected insights into aspects of human relations ("The Motherside", "Performers are Holy").

In an interview for the *ARC* magazine website, King discussed what she perceived to be conflicts among her own roles as poet, mother-about-the-house, and dean. "When I am able to let myself slip totally into poetry mode, I enjoy it," she said. "I feel dreamy and relaxed and cheerful, but I must admit I am totally useless, the house won't be clean and there will be no point expecting me to commit to anything." She continued: "When I am in administrative mode I am really quite efficient and the poet persona annoys me to pieces – and I just can't wear the two different hats and achieve anything at all, I just feel totally pulled apart. When I force myself to do it I find that the best I can get are *Performance Anxiety*–type poems. They are frightening to write and I don't enjoy living in that mode."

But it's the different roles we take on that make us who we are. While King feels a conflict, she is really one actor moving through different scenes. The settings and scenarios might change. But the individual remains the same. "You add to," poet Thom Gunn wrote, "you don't cancel what you do." This is what makes all the world a continuous stage. This is Keats' negative capability.

The performance of roles and their subversion is a theme that also flows in Pamela Mordecai's *Subversive Sonnets* (2012). The very form of these poems embodies the complexity the collection conveys. Many of the poems are sonnets, some in sonnet sequences. All pay careful attention to rhyme, metre, and rhythm, but none are restricted by attention to these devices. The poems encourage us to question the role of the sonnet in contemporary poetry, yet, as a sign of Mordecai's achievement, do not draw overt attention to their form.

The Jamaican poet – who lives in Canada – is also a playwright, and these poems have a conversational tone. They include monologues and carry a range of voices within narratives – including a strong, irreverent Jamaican voice within both lyric and storytelling poems. As well as being alive on the page, the poems clearly invite recital.

The book demonstrates how poetry is a performance genre; the poems also sing against oversimplifications of history, race, gender, and age. We often fall into roles, but Mordecai shows us how arbitrary they can be. Behind them is what Dylan Thomas called "the vast undercurrent of human grief, folly, pretension, exaltation."

Mordecai draws the reader in with humour and vivid imagery. Everyday domestic moments come to life and are sometimes recalled with a winning nostalgia. Often these private moments link, abruptly, with the greater current of history. The reader is caught off-guard, as though the rug has been pulled out from under her feet. Seemingly banal moments dissolve, darkly, into history in outstanding poems, such as "Litany on the Line", "Trois hommes: un rêve", and "Lace Makers".

Slavery and history are powerful currents in the book, as made clear in "Litany on the Line":

> O, lay the ancestors to rest inside
> these cursive curls with litanies.
> Anoint their necks, their ankles, wrists,
> with sacred oil. Put wampum shells upon
> their eyes and set bouquets of trembling
> anemones between their fingers and their toes.
> Sing sankeys, beat the drums to dredge
> up greed, harpoon it like Leviathan
> and beach it where the carrion birds will pick
> its pink meat from its bones. Blessed are you
> buried in this blue dirt. Blessed are you
> who never reached this side. Blessed are you
> who listen as the tribe burbles its grievous news
> across these fibre-optic threads. Blessed are you.

In the truly subversive poem "Thomas Thistlewood and Tom", a slave decides to carry out a cruel punishment forced upon him and his lover with a mindset of relish. Love transforms an act of extreme cruelty into the ultimate expression of the heart. The book's opening poem, "Stone Soup", embodies the refusal of the free individual to accept constraints. The story of how Irene Armond was trapped under the rubble of a tobacco factory after the 1907 earthquake in Kingston, Jamaica, then lived to be 101 years of age, comes to symbolise the power of the human spirit, the female body, and of the seemingly marginal underclass. Other poems celebrate women's capacity for surprise, their refusal to accept roles imposed on them, such as a poem about nuns called "Lace Makers", where

> Mother Luke leans hard on the horn
> of her red Ford – first woman in this whole
> island to drive a conveyance not pulled
> by four-footed creatures. Her long black skirt
> slung in between her knees, beads furled into
> her lap, dark glasses on her white bent nose,
> she drive rough as any crufty truck man...

The poem challenges stereotyped expectations of women, nuns, and white people, showing how identity is complex and fluid.

Whilst poems question the purpose of life's theatre, as in "Counting the Ways and Marrying True Minds", where the poet asks, "What sense in all this coming and going?", poems return, time and again, to the power of love. "Yarn Spinner" ends, "What if you die spinning a thread? Die, yes, but never dead."

The self that is loved may be, like Irene Armond, hard to pin down, but both King's and Mordecai's books tell us life is a stage, a place of shadow and light where roles are played, reversed, and shed as parts in a production with no end.

THOM GUNN'S CARNIVAL

Thom Gunn's poem "The Messenger" starts with a question:

> Is this man turning angel as he stares
> At one red flower whose name he does not know,
>   The velvet face, the black-tipped hairs?

The question tells us what to see: a man, an angel, a flower. Think of a Renaissance painting that includes an angel, no doubt bearing some prophetic message, in front of a window or at the bottom of a shaft of light, bowing to a figure to whom he has been summoned. The angel looks at a flower. But the flower has features that beg more questions. What to make of its redness, its velvety texture, its black hair? Suddenly the scene is no longer a religious Renaissance painting. There is a leap into the sensual:

> His eyes dilated like a cat at night,
> His lips move somewhat but he does not speak
>   Of what completes him through his sight.

Whose eyes? The angel looking down? Or the man looking back up? Whose lips? What are the lips doing? We no longer see a solitary person with a flower. We no longer know who is above and who is below. Instead, two figures are changing roles, and one man is on his knees. The phrase "what completes" is threefold: a fantasy fulfilled, a full insertion, a full climax: "His body makes to imitate the flower / Kneeling, with splayed toes pushing at the spoil." The flower is phallic. The prayer, fellatio.

Contraries gush in Thom Gunn's poems. "The Messenger" is an example at one end of the spectrum of his poetry. Openly gay, he could be explicit in his writing. But here, the reader is asked to fill in the blanks. The result is something that is, paradoxically, more vivid. As Baudelaire said, "That which is created by the mind lives more truly than matter."

We live in an era when queer voices are required to wear their politics on their sleeves – whilst straight voices are not. They are never accused of masking their sexuality in their verse. Mystery is their prerogative not ours. Gunn's understated approach might be dismissed as outmoded, apologetic, a form of hiding. But while visibility is undoubtedly powerful, it's a mistake to dismiss him when he writes in this mode. As anyone who has seen Robert Mapplethorpe's flowers knows, less is more.

Gunn was born in Kent, England, on August 29, 1929, and died in San Francisco on April 25, 2004. His father, Herbert, was a newspaper editor. His mother, Charlotte, was a former journalist who wrote poetry. She killed herself when Gunn was fifteen. He was among those who discovered her body. In adult life, he kept a picture of her, holding him as a baby, over his writing desk. He never escaped her embrace. The biggest risk factor for suicide is a relative who did the same. Though much water had passed under the bridge by the time of his death, at the age of 74, from "acute polysubstance abuse", it is not hard to see a link between Gunn's adulthood and the trauma of his mother's death.

I've always felt that masking reveals more than it conceals. This is a truth those who play mas in Trinidad's Carnival know. A costume – whether an elaborate fantasy of imperial life in Rome or a skimpy bikini with feathers and beads – betrays our choices. Choices say something.

Just as we can see patterns in the poet's life, so too can we find them in the poetry. Over the course of several books, there is a movement from poems, such as "The Messenger", in which sex is suggested and those in which sex is handled plainly (for instance, "The Miracle"). There is also a movement from closed poetic forms to a more relaxed line. Whatever might be said about the death of the author, these dynamics were undeniably shaped by aspects of Gunn's life.

Gunn was not close to his father. His mother's death deprived him of an important source of parental approval. At Stanford, he was taught by Yvor Winters. In Winters, who emphasised rigour and discipline, Gunn found a surrogate. But in the process he cultivated a new fear. Would this surrogate accept his sexuality? (In 1995, Gunn told *The Paris Review*, Winters "would have been *appalled* at the idea that I was queer.")

Gunn's use of traditional forms were a way of pleasing his teacher. In studding the early books with rhyming couplets, carefully calibrated meters, sonnets, and other controlled devices, the poet was vying for acceptance from a parental figure. He was also looking for acceptance in the world of English Letters that was still not gay-friendly, despite a long tradition of queer poets and writers. If Gunn's later books tended to have more free verse, more syllabic verse, more prose poetry, this was a reflection of the poet's increasing confidence. Or, viewed another way, his diminished concern with rejection.

The earlier use of traditional poetic forms performed another function. They gave Gunn a straight jacket, or, to change the metaphor, a means of closing a Pandora's box of unruly emotion. Winters' ideal of discipline could have been a way of keeping self-destructive forces at bay by imposing order on language. Gunn remained HIV negative, but the devastating effects of HIV/AIDS surrounded him. Despite this, it is evident his sexual compulsions never dimmed, even into his 60s and 70s. Nor, it seems, his risk-taking. His partner, Mike Kitay, remarked: "It seemed to me something besides libido. There's something there that's bottomless, that no amount can fill up."

If you look closely at the body of Gunn's poetry you see another transformation. As the years pass, more and more flowers spring from the soil of Gunn's words. Foxgloves, lilies, lilacs, poppies, tulips, morning glories. The red flower of "The Messenger" is just one example. There's a vitality and celebration, even if tempered by the sombreness of work that deals with death.

"Rebellion," Gunn wrote in *The Passages of Joy*, "comes dressed in conformity". He may have been looking for acceptance in his poetry, but he was also doing the opposite. Just as St Lucian poet Derek Walcott co-opted traditional forms to send a message back to the colonial motherland, so too did Gunn deploy formal poetic structures to make a point. In his poetry Gunn says, as a gay man: Look I can do this too, just like any of you. He also says: Look, let us laugh at the quaintness of this masquerade together. In such carnivalesque contrariness lies a sophisticated queerness that is sometimes not fully appreciated. It's a radical inside job.

LANGSTON HUGHES IN TRINIDAD

If Trinidad was on Langston Hughes' radar he certainly kept it quiet. One hint came, however, when in 1940 he was asked to write two pieces for an exposition celebrating the diamond jubilee of Emancipation. In *Tropics After Dark* (a revue which critics regard as slight and which was never mounted), Hughes sets the action on a Carnival night. The cast includes Coloma, a girl from Trinidad, and Buddy, a tourist from Harlem. At one stage Buddy and Coloma meet in Martinique and he sings, "How did I know when I took that cruise/ That I'd lose my heart in Trinidad?"

In real life, Hughes had several ties to Trinidad. Arnold Rampersad's rich, two-volume biography tells us how the poet had at least two Trinidadian loves. While living in Paris he met Anne Marie Coussey, later wife of Hugh Wooding, the future chief justice. And during a trip to Moscow he met Sylvia 'Si-Lan' Chen, a child of the Trinidad-born foreign minister of China, Eugene Chen, and a cousin of the Trinidad-born dancer, Dai Ailian, who became the "mother of Chinese ballet". In New York, he also became acquainted with the dancer Beryl McBurnie, "La Belle Rosette". He corresponded with a number of Caribbean writers, including the Trinidadian poet, Harold M. Telemaque (whose poems "Roots" and "Adina" he included in an anthology). But in November 1959, he did better than correspond.

As part of a Caribbean tour, Hughes spent almost two weeks in Trinidad, delivering a series of free lectures at the Public Library, Knox Street, Port of Spain. Among those present on the night of November 11, 1959, was C.L.R. James, who defied a sudden illness in order to attend (he had been due to preside over the event but instead arrived during a question and answer segment).

On this trip, Hughes met Dr Eric Williams, then premier (Independence was three years away). He also met Derek Walcott, whom he described in a letter as a "very good poet" (Walcott's then fiancée, Margaret Maillard, was, incidentally, a cousin of Sylvia Chen). "Mr Hughes is considered to be the greatest living American poet," said the *Trinidad Guardian* of November 13, 1959. The poet, who depended entirely on his writing to earn a living, and at times lived in near poverty, joked that he might retire.

"One big commercial hit and then I'll come here to live and drink some rum," he mamaguyed. In his lectures, he advised writers to stick to the truth. "An artist must be true to his own integrity," he said. But who Langston Hughes was is the riddle that thousands of pages worth of biography and scholarly publications have been unable to resolve.

In the 48 hours after the 2016 US election, the website of the Academy of American Poets recorded an increase in visitors. There was a surge of tweets and retweets of links to poems on the site. Among the top poems read during the period were Maya Angelou's "Still I Rise" (read more than 50,000 times); Langston Hughes' "Let America Be America Again" (35,000 times) and W.H. Auden's "September 1, 1939" (almost 25,000 times). The victory of Donald Trump seems to have triggered self-searching and a turn to poetry. Even Senator Tim Kaine, in introducing Hillary Clinton, when she made her concession speech, turned to poetry.
    "I'm proud of Hillary Clinton," said Kaine, "because, in the words of Langston Hughes, she has held fast to dreams." Kaine was referring to Hughes' short, sombre poem, "Dreams":

Hold fast to dreams
For if dreams die
Life is a broken-winged bird
That cannot fly.

What are the dreams with which Hughes was concerned? His porous lines allow multiple interpretations. Because it was written by a young black poet during the worst years of Jim Crow in America, it is easy to see the poem as a civil rights rallying-call to urge society to stick to its aspiration for racial equality.
    But one cannot read a poem like this without being aware of the wider idea of the American dream. That is a dream that embraces the idea that any person, no matter their background, can achieve success. Kaine's use of the poem reflects the fact that Hillary Clinton was the first woman to seek the job of president. Hughes' poem is unspecific enough to be all-embracing.
    That Hughes was calling for race and gender equality is something many will readily accept. Yet another kind of advocacy is, for others, problematic. The poem can also be read as about something close to Hughes' heart, perhaps the closest thing to his heart: his sexuality.
    Dreams are situated within an organic world. Nature imagery dominates: birds are in flight, fields grow, snow falls. Dreams, though involuntary, are given a tangible quality: they must be held close and held fast. They are given limbs; they provide sustenance; they die. In our everyday experience, dreams are as often sexual as they are inspirational. Thus understood, Hughes is not only speaking of black and female bodies, he is

also speaking of queer bodies. The problem with this reading is that it is as unprovable as all of the others. It faces the added complication of being counter to how some would prefer to remember this iconic, black, civil rights poet.

His name was not Langston. It was James. When he travelled, he made bookings under the name of James Hughes. While we mark the anniversary of his birth on February 1, there is no formal record of the event. Rampersad put his date of birth at, "near midnight on 1 February 1902" at Joplin, Missouri. But Missouri did not require the registration of infants and it seems the birth was never officially entered. In 2018, poet Eric McHenry found online archive material that suggests that Hughes was born in 1901. The puzzle around his date of birth was a taste of what was to come.

Other puzzles: Hughes was black, but his ancestry was, like most ancestries, mixed: Native American, French and African. Was he or was he not a communist? The question of his sexuality is equally vexed. Despite his amorous correspondence and poems addressed to females, who were presumably romantic interests, Hughes was seen as asexual by some, gay by others.

Rampersad finds no clear evidence in the archives, but that's not surprising. Sexuality is such a fraught thing. How do we define it? By one's actions? Affirmations? Unexpressed but guessed at preferences? Some-times we don't leave evidence behind: there's no paper trail. Even the evidence of an actual sexual act has to be questioned. Do all our actions reveal our innermost impulses?

Still, in the case of Hughes I believe we have enough evidence to assess, with a high degree of probability, that he was gay. He surrounded himself with gay men. Very early on he formed intense attachments to people like Countee Cullen and Alain Locke. In Locke, the chair of the Department of Philosophy at Howard University, Hughes identified a possible benefac-tor, but also developed what was obviously a deep attraction and an awareness of the other man's interest.

"I should like to know you and I hope you'll write to me again," Hughes wrote innocently enough in an early letter to Locke. By April 6, 1923, he was asking his friend, Cullen, "Is Mr Locke married?" Locke was definitely not. In a letter to Locke, sent in May, 1923, Hughes wrote:

> I am going to have some pictures taken this week, (one for Mr. Kerlin's *Negro Poets*) and I shall send one to you. Then if we meet on some strange road this summer we shall recognize one another… Do you like Walt Whitman's poetry? His 'Song of the Open Road' and the poems in 'Calamus'?

The reference to Whitman's homoerotic Calamus sequence would not have gone unnoticed by Locke. In the same letter, Hughes also responds to Locke's disclosure of his plans to visit Germany and the pyramids of Egypt saying, "How wonderful! I wish I were going with you." His flirtation was taken seriously by Locke who, in his next letter, pushed the idea, prompting Hughes to backtrack, saying he would not be available after all, but maybe they might meet "in Piraeus or Alexandria". The possibility was described by Hughes as "delightful and too romantic! But, maybe – who knows?" This flirtation continued as Hughes eyed the possibility of attending Howard. Then, on February 2, 1924, something in Hughes snapped. He sent Locke a telegram: "MAY I COME NOW PLEASE LET ME KNOW TONIGHT." Two days later, Hughes wrote a letter attempting to explain this outburst:

> Forgive me for the sudden and unexpected message I sent to you. I'm sorry. I should have known that one couldn't begin in the middle of the term and that I wasn't ready to come anyway. But I had been reading all your letters that day and a sudden desire came over me to come to you then, right then, to stay with you and know you. I need to know you. But I am stupid sometimes.

Though it was often asserted that Hughes was asexual, it is clear he had sex. He caught a sexually transmitted disease at least once. On one occasion, he even told one of his secretaries that he had had sex with a sailor on a foreign trip. According to Arnold Rampersad's biography, the encounter occurred around 1923 when Hughes was travelling on the *West Hesseltine*. The ship made several stops, including the Azores and Lagos. According to Rampersad, Hughes engaged in "a swift exchange initiated by an aggressive crewman, with Hughes as the 'male' partner". The following dialogue is laid out in the first volume of Rampersad's biography:

> "Won't it hurt you," I said.
> "Not unless it's square," he said. "Are you square?"
> "Could be," I said.
> "Let's see," he said. (p. 77)

Despite the vital nature of this incident to the overall question of Hughes' sexuality, we are given little more. Who is speaking? Where is the event taking place? None of this is disclosed, if it is known. Rampersad concludes that Hughes was probably asexual. He later said, "I was quite willing to reveal that Hughes was homosexual and I certainly went looking for the evidence. But I came up with nothing… But I'm not saying he was not gay. I'm saying the evidence isn't there… It's a complicated business and I don't know where people get off saying he was gay, he was gay, let's claim him."

Yet, the "evidence" Rampersad did not find is there for all to see in his own biography, such as the story of Hughes' encounter with the unnamed sailor, the disclosure of the supposedly asexual Hughes contracting gonorrhoea and Hughes' intense relationships with Locke, Cullen and other males, relationships which cannot be described as solely platonic.

The virtues of Rampersad's biography are many, but he reveals something of his attitudes to gay sexuality when he describes Hughes as being a figure at risk of being "claimed", and the implied negative judgements of the gay figures around Hughes who regarded him as "viable". Here, there is a distinct difference to Rampersad's biography's openness in seeing Hughes in a heterosexual light – telling us he frequented bordellos and prostitutes – itself something of a contradiction to the assertion of Hughes' asexuality.

Hughes was quite possibly a character we know well: someone on the down-low; someone who dated women but who also made room for relationships with gay men, viewing these relationships as strategic; who tells himself he is using these men to advance himself when, in fact, this is a rationalization of an illicit desire he will not acknowledge. Such a person sometimes views gay people as inherently weak and, therefore, in addition to the external social pressures, has a profound incentive not to claim allegiance to the queer. Hilton Als has pointed to the poem "Cafe: 3AM", which takes aim at homophobic police action and sympathises with homosexuals ("God, Nature / or somebody / made them that way"); as well as Hughes' loveless childhood, where he would not have found acceptance. Couple these with social prejudice at the time and the idea of a gay Langston Hughes becomes no mere vogue.

It was the need to ventilate all this that drove me to write the poem, "Langston Hughes in Trinidad: A Closet Drama in Five Scenes" (it appears in *Pitch Lake*). While the issue of Hughes' sexuality has been dealt with in Isaac Julien's beautiful film *Looking for Langston*, I thought it more appropriate to address the poet's sexuality in his own medium, co-opting Heathcote Williams' notion of the investigative poem – a poem that could essay facts and suggest verdicts but without the need for the messy nuances, and uncertainties that adhere to them, of the academic paper. I liked the pun in the term "closet drama" and felt a sequence would yield a kind of investigative poetic meditation. With a few exceptions, each line in the sequence is a fact culled from the publicly available material on Hughes. I felt I owed it to the list of gay men who just so happened to have fallen deeply in love with Hughes, and to Hughes himself, who was obviously labouring under conflicts that are still pertinent to members the LGBT community today.

In sharp contrast to the complex picture of the man is his simple, magnificent poetry. The author of "The Negro Speaks of Rivers", "I, Too", and "The Weary Blues" was influenced by Walt Whitman, gospel and jazz.

He worked tirelessly to advance race equality (which he defined widely, at one point believing India's fate as a nation was tied to it).

He died abruptly, eight years after his Trinidad visit, of complications from prostate surgery. As Rampersad observes, it is impossible to know if race played a role in the quality of his hospital treatment. Be that as it may, at the funeral, mourners played Duke Ellington's "Do Nothing Til You Hear From Me". Perhaps many of those in attendance, listening to Ellington's song about trusting a lover's word, wondered to whom the song was really addressed.

IN THE FIRES OF HOPE AND PRAYER

Look carefully at a poem and you will see flame. This is certainly true of the work of two poets from Trinidad and Tobago who, though long migrated from their homeland, deploy fire imagery to evoke longing and Caribbean identity. Their beautiful poems also work in incendiary, phosphorescent ways – throwing mysterious light into a dark cave. Just as these poems reveal with blinding light, they also create shadows on the walls. As the title of Lauren K. Alleyne's *Difficult Fruit* suggests, they are not easy to pin down. But we are grateful to experience their heat.

Two poems in Roger Robinson's *The Butterfly Hotel* are concerned with deyas, the small clay lamps used in Hindu Divali celebrations. In "Where I'm From", the voice of the poem uses the deya to assert a Trinidadian melting-pot identity: "I am from the flickering flame of a deya, blue at the wick, luminous,/smelling of kerosene". And in "Collage", Robinson describes the making of the small round clay vessel into which oil and wick are placed:

> The gentle curve of a finger and thumb
> in the wet clay make a tiny deya;
> it's beheaded by twine and set aside
> for baking – hardened by fire
> to hold a burning flame.

The deya is a vessel of fire, yes, but even the process of making a deya reveals its purpose. Perhaps, then, this is a metaphor for poetry and art. Other sections of Robinson's collection are concerned with fire. In "Brixton Revo 2011", the poet invokes the London Riots of 2011:

> they ransacked phone shops, darted in and out
> of trainer shops lit by flares of fire.
> As thick black smoke billowed
> from inside they stood still.

The poem is a torrent, fuelled by rage and an unstated history. We are left "smelling the petrol in the air". Then, in the prose poem, "Month One", an immigrant's first impressions are recorded:

He bought chilli peppers from the market and set his tongue aflame.
He spent his last remaining coins on telephone calls home and listened
to static. He kept his heater at the glowing-coal setting... He felt the
warmth of home in the industrial dryers. The windows of washing machines
reminded him of planes.

Fire is home. While we can see the easy link between heat and the
tropics, the observations here feel fresh: washing machines turning
to planes, the choice of food mimicking the desire for a different climate;
showing up a familiar longing. If "Brixton Revo 2011" is concerned
with an escalation into mob behaviour and crime, it connects with "As
All Boys Did", in which a subtle degeneration of behaviour among
children raises questions about the pathways towards violent crime.
The poem opens with a description of casual childish cruelty:

> We knelt and lit
> the flame, protected
> it from the wind as we dripped
> hot wax on the caterpillar.

But later, the stakes get much higher:

> We lit fires in forest hills,
> ran blindly down
> with flames at our heels,
> stole cocoa pods
> from the estate trees,
> ran and laughed
> at the guards' gunshots.

Though fire remains the constant, things have got deadlier. The same
kind of recklessness of outcomes is what links both moments, hinting
at the need to express an interior rage, though in some respects not
expressing rage is worse. In "Texaco Oil Storage Tanks", unemployed
workers, cogs in a global political wheel, are forced to beg "with burning
sun on their shame". Another connection to "Brixton Revo 2011" comes
in "Area", which begins:

> With the halos of our angelheaded
> Afros, we walk like gunslingers. Hipsters
> with thick cardboard dancefloors in our hands,
> we'll be burning crews on their own streets.

At least, here, rage and flame has been transmuted into the art of the
break-dance. All this weaves a kind of incandescent garland around

the book's strong, pastoral pieces. When the smoke clears, we have a sense of seeing the world in a clearer way; our senses are more alert, and we feel the landscapes around us more intimately. "The Immigrant's Lament" ends:

> The snow falls
> like pieces of a crumbling sky;
> he thinks it turns men
> into ghosts.

One poem, "Monarch Exodus", merges the book's different themes and imagery, of migration, flight, fire, risk, determination:

> We won't stop till our journey's done.
> As throngs of us invade the sky
> our countless numbers block the sun.
> And when we move, we move as one
> and few that fly return alive.

We feel a sense of movement, through time and history. Many tribes, flocks, groupings and ideologies – both good and bad – can be read into this piece. It is an achievement.

Lauren K. Alleyne's *Difficult Fruit* contains poems that function in similar ways. It, too, is studded with fire, and Alleyne deploys a wide range of poetic forms – from the sonnet crown to the ghazal – to pitch beauty of form against the ugliness of what is being described. In a poem such as "On the Most Depressing Day of the Year, Jan. 24th", language takes on the qualities of the elemental: a face looms like, "a flaming sentence". In "John White Defends", religion and racism conflagrate: "I wanted / to spare him the burning / crosses". Not only do we see images of the burning crosses of the Ku Klux Klan, but we are made to contemplate structural, institutional forms of bigotry. The entire armature of religion is welded to a larger social problem of Jim Crow and "the whip of a merciless law". Even when located, decades later, in a suburban setting of "petunias and peonies", the voice of the poem still laments: "I should have known / There would be a reckoning". This fire is hard to out.

Nature and illness attack the body in "Elegy", where "the infection flamed through / the kerosene trail of your blood". And with death is love, which "charms good sense / into sweet, burning madness", in 'Love in G Major'. In 'The Edges of Things', "a single longing" sees "lip to whisper / burning to breast", and in "Seven", a memory of a first communion is transformed: "your dress is burning / white, your veil engulfs your head / like lacy flames".

As with Robinson's book, the imagery of fire provides links to other matters in the book. The subject of rape is buried deep within the sonnet crown "Eighteen". That choice of form signals an elaborate apparent cover where the investment in complex form seems to erect a protective cover over a buried truth we would prefer to avoid. It does nothing of the sort, in fact drawing attention to the emotional charge of the experience written about, which has lost nothing of that charge by being shaped into art. A similar idea of subterfuge is raised by the poem "Catching Spy".

In this volume, the seemingly out of place sometimes becomes the centre. Such is the case with the poem "Love in A Flat", in which a single "off"-note by Coltrane becomes the heart of a melody. But while both books share an impulse to engage in strategic and only seeming misdirection, the core of both is a concern with love. In the end, readers are left like Beatrice in Dante's *La vita nuova*, eating from a burning heart.

HIS FATHER'S DISCIPLE

Martín Espada's father refused to sit at the back of the bus. It was December, 1949, in Biloxi, Mississippi. Frank Espada was a dark-skinned Puerto Rican raised in New York. He did not accept Jim Crow laws. His sentence? A week's jail.

Vivas to Those Who Have Failed is a work of advocacy and a monument to that father. The personal and the political are confederated by a poet with a lens as wide as Walt Whitman's. (The book's title comes from section 18 of Whitman's "Song of Myself".)

The title poem sequence, "Vivas to Those Who Have Failed: The Paterson Silk Strike, 1913", deals with an unprecedented six-month strike that marked a pivotal moment in American labour history. Paterson, New Jersey, was an industrial powerhouse. The great falls of the Passaic River fuelled mills and dye houses that produced almost half the nation's silk. But when owners sought to double workload and cut jobs, 35,000 workers mobilised. They sought an eight-hour day and better conditions. The stoppage was initially expected to last weeks; it dragged on for months. In the end, 1,850 workers were jailed, two people died, none of their demands were met.

The location is of particular significance. Paterson has often been associated with the beginnings of the modern United States. William Carlos Williams' famous book-length poem *Paterson* is set there (his sprawling sequence contains references to the strike). The city makes an appearance in Allen Ginsberg's "Howl", and more recently in Junot Diaz's *The Brief Wondrous Life of Oscar Wao*. Espada sees a kind of victory even though the strike failed in its immediate objectives. Vivas in the sense of salute.

The 1913 strike also embodied fault lines that still resonate in American society. The silk workers were largely immigrants, and many supporters of the strike were critics of unbridled profiteering. With the rise of Donald Trump, the Paterson strike remains a potent symbol of the challenges still facing America. Espada sees it as a hopeful, prescient moment: "Vivas to those who have failed: for they become the river". He seeks to remember the unremembered, those "outside history", as Eavan Boland might put it, such as this anonymous protester:

He sat down without another word, sank back
into the fumes, name and face rubbed off
by oblivion's thumb like a Roman coin
from the earth of his birthplace dug up
after a thousand years, as the strikers
shouted the only praise he would ever hear.

In the collection, some poems show history repeating itself. The poem, "The Right Foot of Juan De Oñate", deals with a brutal event during the Spanish settlement of the American West. The conquistador, Oñate, in an act of vengeance for a deadly rebellion by the Acoma Pueblo, sentenced the perpetrators to a cruel punishment: to have a foot cut off. In 1998, a Native American group severed the right foot of a bronze statute that had been erected in Oñate's honour. As with recent events at Charlottesville – which saw deadly racist attacks in reaction to the proposed removal of a statue of the confederate general Robert E. Lee – this action underlined how monuments are like poems: they are more about the present than the past.

In other poems, Espada finds ways of bringing consolation without denying the pain. In "Heal the Cracks in the Bell of the World" – which addresses the 2012 Sandy Hook Elementary school massacre – we are asked to have hope in the way force is transformed into healing: "I was born of bullets, but now I sing/ of a world where bullets melt into bells". In "Ghazal For A Tall Boy from New Hampshire", Espada writes movingly about his student, Jim Foley, the journalist beheaded by ISIS in August 2014. He ties Foley to the fabric of America, working as "a teacher too, teaching in another mill town". Of Foley's students, Espada writes, "In Spanish, they knew him... with him they wrote a poem of waterfalls". All the complex questions that can be asked about Foley's wonderful yet ultimately tragic life are distilled into a slender essence. The poem closes with the lines:

Once he was a tall boy from New Hampshire, standing in my doorway.
He spoke Spanish. He wanted to teach. I knew him. I never knew him.

But amid the book's expressions of hope there is also a sense of weariness over the constant need to resist oppression. This is hinted at in the contrast between the title and the body of Espada's poem about Trayvon Martin. There's the lengthy title, "Chalkboard on the Wall of a Diner in Providence, Rhode Island the Morning After George Zimmerman was Acquitted in the Shooting Death of Trayvon Martin, An Unarmed Black Teenager". There is an epigraph from Martin Luther King, "Injustice anywhere is a threat to justice everywhere". The poem has just one line: "Daily Special: vegetarian chili". It protests the expected poetic treatment of an outrage. The proceedings are cut short just as Trayvon's life was snuffed out.

Poem after poem asks: what is failure? Who gets to define "those who have failed"? The Paterson Silk Strike may have been a failure in the sense that the workers did not achieve their demands. But the show of strength and solidarity becomes an beacon empowering generations to come.

If there is one arena where notions of failure and success sit uneasily it is within art. How do we judge the success of a work of literature? By the extent of its readership? By its critical reception? By the author's personal satisfaction with what she or he set out to do? And at what stage are we ready to carry out these assessments? Upon publication? A year or two after? A decade? A century?

Behind Espada's subversion of notions of success and failure is a complex relationship to religion. The poet's deeply felt advocacy for justice and his veneration of the rituals of protest activity feel almost evangelical. In "The Goddamned Crucifix" he paints a scene involving his father. This time, the firebrand Frank is not protesting racial inequality, but is ill in hospital, seemingly near death. The sick man's one request is for the crucifix in the room to be removed:

> ...so I lifted Jesus off the nail on the wall
> and hid Him in the drawer next to the bed, stuffed
> back down into the darkness before the resurrection.
> Only then did the miracle come to pass: my father lived.

This is a spiritual reward for a renunciation of the spiritual. And if we think further: what could be more paradoxical than the idea that the crucifixion was a triumph, as believers assert? Was the crucifixion not also an act of protest? The poet, protestor and priest meet.

So we are prepared for the subversive cycle of death and resurrection that closes the book. "El Morivivi" is dedicated to the poet's father. It is named after the plant that opens and closes to the touch:

> The furious pulse that fired his heart in every fight flooded
> the chambers of his heart. The doctors scrutinized the film,
> the grainy shadows and the light, but could never see: my father
> was a morivivi. I died. I lived. He died. He lived. He dies. He lives.

YOU CAN SEE VENEZUELA FROM TRINIDAD

What do an Old Fashioned, a Daiquiri, and a Manhattan have in common? One ingredient: Angostura Bitters – one of those things you either know about or you don't. If you're from Trinidad, you know about it.

Trinidadians put bitters in everything. And I mean everything. From an early age, children see their parents sprinkling it on meats, adding it to cakes, even dashing it on top of coconut ice-cream. From young we recognise the bottle, with its yellow cap and an old-fashioned paper label bearing the coat of arms of the British royal family. Angostura has held a warrant of appointment from Buckingham Palace since 1955.

Along with steelpan music, the bitumen from the Pitch Lake, and the cricketer Brian Lara, Angostura Bitters is one of Trinidad's more famous gifts to the world – a continuing source of pride and patriotism. Perhaps this is why few will acknowledge that, while quintessentially Trinidadian, Angostura Bitters is actually Venezuelan.

And German, too.

It was first made in the town called Angostura in Venezuela. The town was later renamed Ciudad Bolivar, but the bitters kept its maiden name. As legend has it, it all started in 1824 when Dr Johann Siegert first produced aromatic bitters as a medicinal tincture designed to alleviate stomach problems. Siegert's family had moved to Venezuela from Germany in 1820 to serve as surgeon-general in Simon Bolivar's army. In the 1870s, Dr Siegert's three sons migrated to Trinidad, bringing Angostura with them. They thrived, becoming owners of an estate in the capital. Today, Carlos, Luis and Alfredo have streets of the city named after them. Not far from the main drinking and recreation hub of the capital, there is a square commemorating the Siegert family.

The story of Angostura Bitters is emblematic of the history of Trinidad and Tobago itself. Many who today live in the two islands have come from elsewhere, and I refer here to those who came after the arrival of enslaved Africans and indentured Indians in the 18th and 19th centuries. So it is baffling to witness the aggressive xenophobia that is greeting the wave of Venezuelan immigrants coming to the island, fleeing the government of Nicolas Maduro. In a blind rage, Trinidadians have fallen prey to amnesia, forgetting the long history of two-way traffic across the Gulf of Paria, forgetting a shared colonial history, forgetting that the land upon which they walk is, geographically, a part of the Venezuelan mainland. The middle name of Simon Bolivar, the great Venezuelan liberator, was Trinidad. Both the man and the island were named after the same thing: the Holy Trinity.

In the year 2019, such nuances were jettisoned in Trinidad as protesters, opposed to the government granting Venezuelans amnesty, gathered on a balmy June night in Woodbrook, a stone's throw away from Siegert Square, to make known their displeasure at the rising number of Latinos in the country.

"Close the border!" they cried. Confusingly, some members of the protest seemed of two minds. They considered going home to sleep in their beds. The protest organisers had to take to their megaphones to convince these doubting Thomases: "You have to stay! The world must know we sleep on the ground for our country; the country must know how many of us sleep on the ground to stand up and fight, because that is how they will join us." In this case, the flame didn't grow. The group remains at about 100 strong in a country of 1.3 million people.

Venezuelans, too, took to protesting in Trinidad. They gathered outside the offices of the United Nations to complain about police heavy-handedness. They went on hunger strikes at an immigration detention centre for better medical care. They gathered in the town of Aranguez, whose name harks back to Trinidad's past as a Spanish colony, to call on the authorities to enforce international laws relating to refugees.

"Every day we are insulted and threatened," they lamented. Venezuela's misfortune has injected another noise into Trinidad's troubled democracy.

Like his predecessor Hugo Chavez, Nicolas Maduro also turned up in Port of Spain. He visited the president and prime minister. He went on a charm offensive, asking Trinidadians and Venezuelans to "make love", thereby bringing the countries closer. His reception, over the course of several visits, was mixed. At one stage a group of about thirty local socialists protested in support of him, while a similarly small group, led by a psychic, protested against him. For a while, the government supported Maduro, then the opposition announced support for Juan Guaido.

To announce their arrival, Venezuelans in Trinidad launched a Carnival band. Speaking in hesitant English, they expressed a fervent desire to create "meaningful costumes". It was as though they had come home. If there is a difference between Venezuelan mas and Trinidad mas it's hard to tell. The band's costumes looked exactly like all the other Carnival costumes: bikinis, beads and feathers. Venezuelans have become Uber drivers, popped up on Tinder and Grindr, joined the National Drama Association.

Before the current influx of refugees, Venezuelans would come in through Cedros port in the south of Trinidad, taking the day to shop in bulk for goods that were in short supply in Caracas. Then, that port was closed. But the Venezuelans, through mysterious means, continued to come. A group of hundreds were found in a forest, living off mangos.

But though Spanish is taught in schools, the language barrier for English-speaking Trinidadians has proved stronger than geography. What Venezuelans like to eat, what they wear, what they watch on TV, how they like to party – the average Trinidadian is none the wiser. The same applies to the 32 million Venezuelans' knowledge of the island. Some even mistake Trinidad as just another part of their country.

Perhaps the estrangement is a hangover from the past. As suggested by scholar Jak Peake, there was something of a "historic, linguistic and administrative cleavage from Venezuela – initiated by Trinidad's capture by the British from Spain in 1797." Yet, "before its capture by the British in 1797, Trinidad might have been attached, as it was under Spanish colonialism, to Venezuela, or the huge area that formed the Viceroyalty of New Grenada."

At least some aspects of Trinidad's collective consciousness – its nineteenth and twentieth-century literatures – have glanced across the Gulf of Paria to the mainland. Peake gives examples like E.L. Joseph's *Warner Arundell* (1838), the anonymous novel *Adolphus* (1853), Michel Maxwell Philip's novel *Emmanuel Appadocca* (1854), C.L.R. James' short story "Revolution" (1931), Ralph de Boissière's *Crown Jewel* (1952), Earl Lovelace's short-story "Joebell and America" (1988), Lawrence Scott's *Witchbroom* (1993), his short story "Chameleon" (1994), Dionne Brand's *At the Full and the Change of the Moon* (1999), and Robert Antoni's *My Grandmother's Erotic Folktales* (2000).

Venezuelan literature, too, has returned the furtive glance. Peake notes that Rómulo Gallegos, the first freely elected president of the country, wrote a novel called *Canaima*, published in 1935, in which Trinidad is a reference point. That Trinidad would be a presence in the mind of a man destined to become Venezuela's first, albeit doomed, leader (he was ousted after nine months), was only natural. Long before Chavez and Maduro, the history of Venezuelan politics has always featured Trinidad. For example, Manuel Gual, who along with José María España launched the first conspiracy against colonial rule in 1797, was reportedly poisoned by a Spanish spy in Trinidad in 1800. He died in St Joseph, at the heart of the island.

In contemporary Trinidadian culture there are reminders of the links once dramatised by its literature and once made manifest in real-life political intrigue. Parang music, named after the Spanish word *parranda*, which means a spree or a fête, is performed at Christmas in concerts and in neighbourhoods from door to door. A form of folk music which some say came from Venezuela, it flourished because of Trinidad's proximity to the Spanish mainland. The eating of pastelle, which Venezuelans call *hallaca*, is another Trinidadian Christmas tradition. Trinidadian newspaper columnist Paulo Kernham has noted that Venezuelans were still settling in Trinidad long after the British took control in 1797. Coco panyols, he said in a column at the height of the immigration crisis, worked the cocoa estates.

"What would Christmas be without pastelles?" Kernham implored.

In one thing, however, Trinidadians and Venezuelans are united. Both are obsessed with the Miss Universe pageant. Both countries frequently appear in the top ten. Both have fanatics who follow the pageant religiously. Though often rivals, both countries look at each other with a kind of begrudging respect. Venezuela has won six times, Trinidad and Tobago twice.

Discussions about life in Trinidad and Tobago are often overly simplistic. Them versus us. Inside versus outside. Local versus foreign. What is ignored is that Trinidadians are migratory creatures. A significant minority of the current Trinidad population came from somewhere else in the Caribbean. All of us, except those of Amerindian heritage, came from somewhere else. There is probably a Trinidadian living in every country in the world, present at the site of every national disaster, in the backdrop to every momentous event in history. We leave Trinidad as much as we love it.

Those who stay are part of a population which has, over centuries, been shaped by global events. Just as powerful economic forces across the Atlantic Ocean brought our diverse population to these islands, so too is the destiny of the current population shaped by international developments like the price of oil, the climate crisis, and trade battles between the USA and China. On the one hand we regard the foreign as something to be venerated, on the other hand, as something to be despised – as though we are not already inextricably bound up with the peoples of the Earth.

Our attitude to Venezuela is a good example of this backward thinking. The way people talk about migration is another. One artist recently remarked, "I've spent considerable periods of my life outside of Trinidad, and when I return home I'm always overwhelmed by how unique and precious our culture is. We often look to imitate the outside world, forgetting that what we have to offer is something that no one else can truly replicate." The very language the artist used to express these trite sentiments undermined her point. English did not originate in Trinidad. It is an import.

Just as we are blind to our complex ties, we have an inability to see our deeper problems. While protesters were lining the streets, making an exclusive claim to the territory, bodies were piling up in Trinidad and Tobago's lone state morgue. Billions are spent annually to fight crime, but the murder rate per capita is one of the highest in the world. The economy, driven by oil and gas, is distorted by government subsidies and controls; urban planning is virtually nonexistent; our infrastructure is disintegrating; if you're not rich opportunities are hard to come by; technological development lags. We have produced Nobel-prize winning authors and many persons of high international standing. But such brilliance has done little to improve the country. We have a world-famous Carnival, but it has long been eclipsed by others in charm and novelty.

It is understandable why Venezuelans, who have had to contend with far worse, would want to come here. But the cynic in me thinks it's a mystery why Trinidadians would want to fight for sole proprietorship of the territory. This cynic thinks that Trinidad is a society fixed in its ways, with rigid systems of privilege designed to give more power to those who already have it, and keep entire classes of people effectively disenfranchised. This occurs through the co-option of the political process, itself designed to keep a tight grip on the island's future by erasing what we should learn from the past. Erased today is the knowledge that in 1852 a group of about 700 Trinidadians, enthralled by romantic ideas about Venezuela, left Port of Spain for Caracas. According to Peake, the venture failed as this party met with hostility on the mainland. History repeats.

From Trinidad, you can see Venezuela. But from Trinidad, Trinidadians can't even see themselves.

THE RIGHTEST PLACE

Take a conch shell, insert a strobe light. A tyre, coat with beans. Two starfish, put on an oil drum. A ton of beach sand, ship to a gallery.

This is the artist Blue Curry's way of questioning what belongs where, and maybe *who*.

"I came to London a little over twenty years ago on the casual invite of my aunt who emigrated back in the 60s," he said. "I came for a short visit and never left! I consider London my base and I do feel that I have become a Londoner but the Bahamas is still home."

Curry takes objects from the places where they belong and puts them into another. It's little wonder then that migration is a key part of his story. He was born in Nassau, Bahamas, in 1974. As a child, he would visit the beach with his mother and sister; his father had a barbershop in the business district. The latter became an equally important setting: a social meeting point that brought together top Bahamian politicians and fishermen. "A haircut side by side equalised their positions for a few minutes and conversations that weren't possible anywhere else happened there," he reported. Pursuing that sense of possibility, Curry headed to London where he obtained a BA (Hons) in Photography and Multimedia at the University of Westminster in 2004, then an MFA in Fine Art at Goldsmiths College, London in 2009, making an appearance in the two-part BBC Four documentary "Goldsmiths: But Is It Art?" (2010).

Art that is compelling is often art that is hard to describe. Even Curry has, on occasion, had difficulty explaining what he's doing with his sculptural assemblages, installations, and found poems. In the 2010 documentary he struggled to give the filmmakers a mission statement. "You have this idea of a sculptor or painter just slaving away at this massive canvas, but if the conceptual artist just puts that rock on top of a piece of paper you can't see the labour involved with that and so therefore it's not an artwork," he said. "It's a funny thing to try to explain exactly what a strobing conch shell is saying. What's happening here? I don't know." In the years since, however, others have not been as tongue-tied.

"Dichotomies are at constant play in the work," said designer Melanie Archer in a 2010 profile in *The Caribbean Review of Books.* She detected a sense of fun alongside an "impossible elegance". Art critic Carlos Suarez De Jesus positioned the pieces as balanced on a "tightrope between cultural artifact and tourist souvenir", while Benjamin Genocchio, writing in the *New York Times*, described one of Curry's creations as "satisfying and silly at the same time".

"I'm less concerned nowadays about *how* people engage with my work but that they engage, full stop," Curry said. "Strong juxtapositions of seemingly contradictory ideas and materials can make people engage. Whatever people take from it – fascination, confusion, anger, delight, amusement – boredom is never an option with my work."

Semiotics is the study of signs and how they work. This involves looking at two things: what is signified or communicated, and what does the signifying or communicating (Ferdinand de Saussure). But some see signs in terms of finer categories. For Charles Sanders Peirce, there are three types: icons, indexes, and symbols. An icon resembles what it represents. An index has a direct link to what it depicts (a puddle on the floor is a sign of rain). A symbol has no apparent connection at all to what it signifies, but we agree as a society what it represents (we all concur that a green light at a traffic stop means go). Blue Curry's work is a carnival of icons, indexes and symbols. His installations involve the scrambling of signs concerning race, gender, class, and nationality; they are concerned with the Caribbean, the colonial, and the neo-colonial.

And so with *Untitled* (2010) two starfish are placed, as if dancing or in amorous embrace, on top of an oil drum. There's some frothy silver tinsel between them; mirrored perspex appears to have become their dance floor. The starfish is an easily recognised symbol of the seaside, one of the joyful things we associate with the marine environment. Placing two astride an oil drum is a harsh juxtaposition that makes us confront the environmental impact of oilrigs and fossil fuel usage on this same marine environment.

The mirror gives you the feeling that the starfish are walking on water, another symbolic gesture (or action code, as Roland Barthes might call it) which deepens the sense of their estrangement from where they should be. It also adds a teleological twist: they are Christ-like figures about to be sacrificed. The green colour of the barrel is yet another ironic symbol, green being the colour we associate with nature. Oil itself is natural, even if its harvesting has brought us to a most unnatural climate emergency.

All of this brings us to a place where we must confront the dynamics of how smaller states are affected by the actions of larger, multinational groups, whether conglomerates or countries, in their quest to exploit natural re-sources – the dynamic that has been the lynchpin of the relationship between developing countries and more developed states for centuries.

If *Untitled* (2010) is about the interplay of forces within nature and history, *Souvenir* (2014) is about politics impinging on the human body. The piece is a sculpture comprising four translucent hair combs arranged on a perspex plinth. By their use, combs are both indexical signs of how we tame hair to fit our ideas of beauty and symbols that are emblematic of larger, more oppressive social ideas. In a world where black bodies are made to bow down to white standards of beauty, the comb is a reminder of the painful process by which a mother might try to iron out the kinks in her black daughter's curly hair. Curry, whom some would regard as white within a Caribbean setting, understands his nebulous place within the racial dynamics of the region: that the combs are colourless becomes a powerful gesture of solidarity. For a residency at Alice Yard in Woodbrook, Trinidad, two years later, the artist returned to this subject, this time making a group of assemblages from colourful Afro combs. (Comb sculptures, in fact, have been a longstanding part of his oeuvre, going as far back as 2010.)

Nor does the politics of class escape Curry's gaze. In another untitled piece from 2010, he fills a cement mixer with 30 litres of sunscreen. The cement mixer is a symbol of construction work, of builders, of tough, hardy, typically male figures who might have little concern for skincare regimes. The sunscreen is just like the starfish: a symbol of beach-going, of leisurely life. The work is therefore a paradox heightening the estrangement between two class worlds.

The idea of the male is also present in 2018's *Untitled, Swimsuits, Showerhead*, but by its dramatic absence. Twelve (another signifier: there are twelve disciples, twelve moon cycles, twelve hours on the clock) bathing suits are hung on showerheads lined against a white wall. Bathing suits are, again, symbols of leisure, but these, arranged in this way, suggest something mercenary, perhaps prostitution. The artist might see tourism as a negative thing, but there's also a deep critique of the place of women in society. The limp suits, hung up, seem fetishlike, on display, lined up for an off-stage (likely) male gaze. Their very proliferation speaks to the absence of women in other more "serious" realms of Caribbean society. Women are numerous on the beach, but missing elsewhere, such as in the legislative chamber where females comprise only about 12% of the Bahamas parliament.

"Art doesn't have to say anything but it has to do something," Curry has said. "Art has to transform or rearrange material or ideas in a way that hasn't been seen before; it should complicate the familiar elements of the culture around us and perhaps make us reconsider our position in it." Of *Untitled, Swimsuits, Showerhead* he stated, "I'm asking that these bathing suits, which might seem quite innocuous, be considered in terms of the mental subjugation of Caribbean people. At the same time, because of their ordinary nature as consumer items, they are underestimated as material for sculpture and art, so I am also interested in repositioning them as such."

But another kind of repositioning is occupying Curry's attention these days, with his opening of a new collaborative space in London. He said, "I want it to have a unique and flexible mix of uses, including exhibitions, talks, workshops, socials, community projects and an artist-in-residence programme to name a few." It's a new dawn, located at 250 Morning Lane, London. Besides the obvious symbolism of the address, the space was once the site of a barbershop, bringing Curry full circle to his childhood. Its first exhibition was of work by the Trinidadian painter and designer Bruce Cayonne, known at home for his distinctive fete-signs. Cayonne had made a series of hand-painted typographic works experimenting with the nascent Ruby Cruel identity or brand.

"I see Ruby Cruel as a sort of alter ego, or better put, an anti-ego," Curry said. "It has little to do with my own individual artistic career and more to do with working with others and creating creative possibilities and networks in general." Those networks straddle two seemingly disparate but, in fact, heavily interlinked worlds: the Caribbean and London.

"I get back twice a year and bounce around the Caribbean quite a bit working on various projects," Curry told me. "In two decades I feel as though I've lived through three different London's – which is hard to explain – but art, fashion, music, and attitudes have progressed and changed so many times since I've lived here. The city is not the same one as when I first arrived."

"Just as there are challenges in operating from a small island space, there are challenges to working in a big city. I'm fortunate enough that I can move between the two. This has become intrinsic to the work I make and also to my own identity as a Caribbean person."

Blue Curry and his work might stand out wherever he goes, but he clearly fits in at many different places. The ultimate irony, however, is that by habitually making things seem out of place, by pushing them across boundaries, he makes them belong. Suddenly, they seem in the rightest place, destined for his designs all along.

AN ESSAY INTO THE POETRY of SJ FOWLER, a VISUAL POET and the organiser of the POEM x BRUT reading series in LONDON & THEREABOUTS

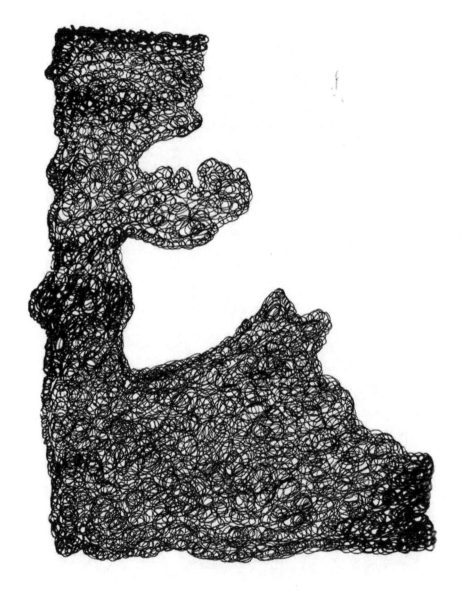

In truth all poetry is visual, all words
are visual (Ezra Pound thought the
Chinese words for tree and sun looked
like what they represented, but we need
not agree with Pound we need only
acknowledge language as a formed system
which we look at to understand) so
visual poetry is a misnomer. Except,
perhaps, if the intention is to heighten
the sense of the visual. To ignite
resistance. To put down the cross of
words and take up the freedom of flight.
To raise the volume on the image, the
hand-held, the human, and mute the word-
processed text (well, maybe not mute but
rather lower) to create what Paul
Hawkins calls prote(s)xt. Fowler's Poem
Brut collaborative series is a human
sculpture in which the parts are played
by poets: installation art that turns
the poetry reading inside out, upending
authoritarian expectations, up heaving
the order imposed by lectern, by podium,
by stage, showing the audience to be
truly complicit in reconciling each poet
with their work and the other poets and
the other readings and the exhibitions
and the theatre of what has occurred and
will occur. This has always been poetry.
Ask the Greeks, with their pattern poems
shaped like axes. Ask William Blake, who
engraved God, heaven and hell.

THE SECRET LIFE OF A DYSLEXIC CRITIC

One day you see the banners. And the posters. And the table with volunteers. It's Dyslexia Week. You pick up a flier listing the symptoms.

√   Difficulty reading, including reading aloud
√   Slow and labour-intensive reading and writing
√   Problems spelling
√   Avoiding activities that involve reading
√   Mispronouncing names or words, or problems retrieving words
√   Trouble understanding jokes or expressions that have a meaning not easily understood from the specific words (idioms), such as "piece of cake" meaning "easy"
√   Spending an unusually long time completing tasks that involve reading or writing
√   Difficulty summarizing a story
√   Trouble learning a foreign language
√   Difficulty memorizing
√   Difficulty doing math problems

They say if you have some of these symptoms you should get screened. You have all of them. You have one of those moments when suddenly everything comes rushing towards you, like a scene in one of those movies where the main character realises who the murderer really is, or finds the cure to the illness, or figures out how to defeat the super-villain – you know the "ah ha!" moment – and you have to get screened NOW, RIGHT AWAY, FORTHWITH, so you go up to one of the volunteers and demand the address of the nearest doctor who can do this sorcery. (*What was written on the volunteer's T-shirt? Don't remember, but the colour was purple.*) You call and make the appointment. You find the place online, do some internet searches about the doctor and turn up for the appointment.

The testing takes longer and is weirder than you expected. The doctor asks you question after question, makes you do exercise after exercise. It feels like being poked and prodded and you get frustrated because sometimes you can do what he asks, but sometimes you can't remember where the red cube was on the poster he just held up; don't know where the bunch of grapes was either, and you really have no idea where the eagle has flown off to. You feel helpless. You realise you're doing badly. But some of the things are easy. In the end, he writes up a report.

There is good news and bad news. The good news is you're not completely useless as a human being, you just have an issue. The bad news is that issue. For someone with your capabilities, you're rather crap at memorising things (*Man, this essay is taking forever to write, water break, have your after dinner snack, eat the banana bread; it has chia seeds and chocolate chips – it's still kinda healthy, right?*) but now, at least, you know the nature of the problem. You can explain the gap between what you say in tutorials and what you write in examinations; you can identify the factors that make things worse – and the factors that make things better. You can manage the situation (*Manage, such a good word*) so yes. So all is not lost because you know that while it's harder for things to get into the bottle, once they are in, they stay in. You have to work harder at things, but it just means you value words more. And you value your memories more, the good and the bad.

As the years go by after the diagnosis, your relationship with reading becomes like your relationship with the sea. At first things are simple. There is an innocence as you dive in, swimming through the velvety water of Carenage, skinny dipping with cousins, looking for urchins underwater. Then, as working life takes over, the sea becomes a minefield. Pack the water cooler, pack the beach chairs, walk with the sun block, walk with the mat, walk with something to put the wet clothes in, choose a good towel, choose a good change of clothes, wear a T-shirt to cover your belly because all the guys seem to like to expose themselves and you're still coming to terms with other human bodies and the representation of self and the idea of The Male. You know you're expected to live up to – *no, conform* – to certain bodily standards (*Is it time for a new paragraph?*), but you don't want to conform, or you can't. You walk with the food, you walk with the extra water, you walk with a book in case you're bored and you have time to read, but you are told not to read in bright sunlight – it's bad for your eyes. Maybe you can have some music, so you walk with the Walkman, the old iPod and the iPod Touch. Reading becomes like this for you, fraught with preparation.

You have to chose the right chair. The room has to be at the right temperature. There must be a certain quality of lighting. It helps to be alone in case you need to read sentences aloud. You get books with larger print. Then you get the electronic version of the book. That way you can increase the font, change the background colour. You know an electronic version of the text is useful because you can also take it with you on the treadmill. Reading on the treadmill helps; the exercise somehow distracts the brain, keeps the noise level in your mind low enough for you to hear the words.

People can actually tell how much you've been reading based on how slim you've become; your brawn is a direct reflection of your imbibing of the great works of literature. You discover audio books, but that's like diving into the deep end of something you can't see the bottom of. You download several epics, but after a promising start with Ovid, things peter out.

Because dyslexia is not a reflection of intelligence, things get tricky. Everybody distrusts you. You're too smart to have made such a simple mistake, they say. How could you write that? If you make a mistake with spelling or mix up the sequence of something or err in the transcription of three-hours of a long garrulous recording the day after a tiring event, someone will go out of their way to call, email, text, to let you know you've made a mistake. They know you'd want to know in order to do it better. They want the best for you, after all. You're a nightmare for editors who know you, who once regarded you as reliable and, therefore, assumed your copy would be clean, only to discover, too late, it's not always so. You know there are things called proofreaders; you know there is a spell check, you know to check and re-check, read and reread, yet you also know people are human. You know mistakes are like the moss piglets, aka water bears, on the moon; they can survive anything, can hunker down and survive radiation and vacuums.

They're always sneaking through, these simple mistakes. There for their, canvas for canvass, spare for spear, 1996 for 1969. You celebrate when you find typos in books like *The Adventure of Tom Sawyer* and *The Bell Jar*. If it could happen to Twain and Plath, it could happen to anybody, you gloat. Besides, your errors are minor. They don't affect the reader's understanding off the overall meaning.

But tell that to the suffering artist. Tell that to a fragile ego. Tell that to the PR officials who have carefully calibrated the optics of these artists' supremely important cultural masterworks – the people whose entire lives have now been disfigured because of your misplaced comma. You've reported on many things in your life. You know people think lowly of the media: expect errors to be made. You've seen a whole industry spring up involving the issuing of pre-action protocol letters by lawyers over typos. You know their clients are governments, constitutional bodies, powerful multinational corporations. All are preferable to dealing with artists who are given society's permission to be unhinged.

Still, you prefer to review visual art. You avoid reviewing novels as much as you can. You like to read the novels you review and that poses a problem. A big problem. You know a good reviewer should have some familiarity with the previous works of the same author. You understand the need to know where the work fits, to assess the book's larger context. A review of one book is never a review of one book. Unless you're reviewing someone who wrote only one book like Harper Lee with *To Kill a Mockingbird* or Ralph Ellison with *Invisible Man* or Boris Pasternak with *Doctor Zhivago* or Margaret Mitchell with *Gone With the Wind* or Emily Bronte with *Wuthering Heights (Wait did Harper Lee really write only one book? Well at least before* Go Set a Watchman; *read Wikipedia page of* Go Set a Watchman; *it was a first draft of* Mockingbird *so really it shouldn't count should it? Look at the clock, listen to the night sounds outside: frogs, birds, crickets. By the way, did Charlotte not destroy the rest of Emily's writing? Maybe Emily wrote more and we just haven't found it yet. Play Kate Bush's "Wuthering Heights", play Kate Bush's "Running Up That Hill", play Stevie Nicks "Edge of Seventeen". Start dancing. Tell dog not to worry about said dancing. Look up the next contact improvisational dance class, look up the next yoga class).*

At one point you read a book about "speed-reading" and it tells you to swallow sentences in whole clauses, break up the line into consumable units, take in as many words at once as possible.

You go back to your university days when you had tomes and tomes to read and had to sink or swim. You remember how you devised strategies to cover as much ground as possible without reading every single thing. You know that's what other people do. But the devil is in the detail. You have to stay as alert as possible, suck up as much as you can.

You marvel at the famous story of Thackeray sitting beside the fireplace reading *Jane Eyre* in one afternoon (*Search to confirm if you read this story somewhere. Wait, where is your* Jane Eyre? *Look for your* Jane Eyre. *Can't find it. Did you lose it when moving between apartments? Loaned it to someone? Vow to never lend a book to anyone again*). You are in awe of the person who tells you they read Eleanor Catton's *The Luminaries* in one go, how they spent "the night" with Marlon James' *A Brief History of Seven Killings*. You know people say they have read things when they haven't. You also know people say they have read things when they *have*. You know there are some books that are just plain difficult to read, that really do take a long time. You consider Catton's complaint about *The Bostonians*, for instance, a book she admires. At the same time, you feel left behind. You feel all these people, all these professional reviewers and editors and publishers out there have the magic ability to sit down at their desks and read tons of books and curate things and come up with clever themes and podcasts and contributions to festival panels too, on top of everything!

You know as a writer it's your job to read as much as you can. Yet look at you: binge-watching *Stranger Things* on Netflix over the weekend with your boyfriend. Shame on you. You develop a deep Catholic guilt about reading (*Would it be too rude to say you have a filthy thought at this moment? Minimise the word processor, and almost pull up the internet browser to satisfy the sudden urge. Think better of it – restraining your impulses to an admirable degree. Now get back to this literary endeavour mindful that your readership, O your dear readership, awaits. Wait, what were you saying again? Oh yes…*) and so you try to tell more and more people you're dyslexic; you join the Dyslexia Association of Trinidad and Tobago; you share their posts on social media.

But when you tell people you're dyslexic the reaction tends to be an eye roll, or they stare back at you with a blank face, either not caring, or not convinced. You learn people don't take dyslexia seriously, or they put it in the file where they put things like "mental health" and "things that are fashionable these days". If they are charitable, they say something like "but you're not giving yourself enough credit". And generally, the whole coming out thing is really kind of useless, because you know they're not going to look at you differently, even though you feel, with the weight of mountains, so different. (*Can I get readers to feel what it feels like, can I replicate that claustrophobia that kicks in, how the words rush at you and it's hard to process it all?*)

You decide you're fed up of this struggle. You are going to master this. You decide to push yourself to read all the books you've been meaning to read for years. Start short. Start with Harold Sonny Ladoo's novel, *No Pain Like This Body*. It's an unforgettable but weird poem, you feel. Continue with anything that's to hand. You just want to get your brain in a rhythm, you just want the muscle to be exercised, you just want reading long things to become second nature. You come to a huge book, a book you would normally avoid like the plague. You take a deep breath and decide, yes, you are ready to review Marlon James' *Black Leopard, Red Wolf*. You fall under its spell. When you finish its 600-plus pages, you love it for reasons related to the text and for reasons not related to the text. You don't want to stop. You continue. No, you don't revert to your customary slim volumes of poetry. You stick to prose.

You start keeping a book diary – a simple list of everything you've read. You choose to write this essay. You want to make this declaration here for everybody to see. The next book you are going to read is *Vanity Fair*. Probably a foolish declaration for several reasons, but you type on anyway. You know that when this essay is published, someone will come up to you and ask: Did you finish *Vanity Fair*? You think the shame, the mortification, the utter humiliation of having to tell people no will motivate you like never before, prodding you with thoughts of Thackeray rolling in his grave waiting for you to finish his book, to reach that last line (*Suddenly remember* Vanity Fair *was your geography teacher's favourite novel; he was your favourite teacher, he also wrote books, many books. Glance at a bookshelf, find the section of the shelf devoted to his tomes, pick up one, open it – come back to this essay later*).

WHAT HAPPENED ON DECEMBER 21, 2019

It begins, really, on December 6 when I decide I'll do this; it begins in my mind as I try to anticipate what shape the day will take and somehow, as the weeks slide by, life aligns with my visions the way the sea, as chaotic as it is, moves to a hidden logic; it begins, though a day never really "begins" since it has no true start, no middle, and no end because what's a day anyway if not an arbitrary designation of time – and don't the philosophers say there is no time without man? For now, let's say it begins, ostensibly, at 06.22 when I wake up; or maybe it begins, truly, at 06.30 when I make a note in my journal to the effect that I've woken up. I get out of bed. I free Chaplin from his crate. I put on his collar. I use the bathroom, weigh myself. I open the laptop to write more notes. Wild noises, parrots outside. Sunlight.

I take Chaplin for a walk. On the way home, two dogs jump over a wall and try to attack him. I hold him in my arms and run into our yard. I read the news. More people have died. I exercise. I feed Chaplin leftover lasagna. I worry about whether we're spoiling Chaplin. I water the plants. It's Saturday so you sleep late. You wake up, we kiss. I read *Robinson Crusoe* because one of the things I'm working on is an essay on *Robinson Crusoe*. I shower, dress, fold laundry. We have a fight over the aesthetics of the antlers we're using to top our Christmas tree. The struggle is real: you want all-silver, I want slivers of gold. Eventually, we make up and kiss. I eat breakfast. Oatmeal. We go to an arts and craft store. We go to the mall. We have lunch in the mall. I have coo coo, callaloo, beets. You have three types of deep-fried chicken. On the way home, the rain falls and we can't see. In the car, I remember playing in the rain as a child, playing with water as a child, playing in the yard as a child, getting soaked, my school uniform sticking to my body, cold and damp, but how sweet the rain smelled. When we get home we have a nap. I wake up and it's like a new day. I finish *Robinson Crusoe*. We finish the antlers. We get gyros for dinner. The guy mixes up my order. On the way home, you lose your slipper in a drain, have to walk home half-barefoot.

We get ready for a Christmas party happening tonight. There's some discussion about what exactly a "festive chic" dress code means. Fabian comes over. Jeevan comes over. Rohan comes over. We have shots, eat chips, prawn crackers. We talk about life, talk about men, hope the party will be a sausage fest. The party's at an art gallery around the corner so we walk. The gallery is half-empty. We drink sorrel mojitos, commiserate over the lack of people to flirt with. The DJ plays the Electric Slide song and that's the last straw. We go to the bar downstairs, where things are quiet as well. We decide we'd be better off back home, liming around the kitchen table. When we get home you have an idea: we should go to a gay fete that's also happening tonight. We agree, but some of us need to change first. I'd planned to write this at the end of the day, so that the exercise to write what happens on a particular day would include the act of writing – a kind of infinity mirror. I'll write it tomorrow, I say to myself. The clock is about to strike midnight. We head out, yet again, into the night.

BORIS JOHNSON IN THE EYES OF A POET – A VERSE ESSAY

1.

Heathcote Williams was an actor, a playwright,
a painter, a sculptor, a magician,
a naturalist who scoured the Amazon

for honey-producing wasps, a polymath,
and a poet whose last book was on
Boris Johnson. Of Johnson, Williams wrote:

the politician had campaigned to restore
foxhunting, described Ugandans as "piccaninnies",
Chinese workers "puffing coolies", argued for

the resumption of colonialism,
opposed the Kyoto Treaty on climate
change, supported the homophobic Section 28,

compared civil partnerships to "three men and
a dog" getting married, scrapped, as mayor
of London, plans to make half of all new

homes cheap enough for ordinary London
workers, opposed the ban on smoking, backed
the Iraq War, fabricated stories

when he was a reporter, supplied details
of another reporter to a person
who wanted to harm that reporter. The

name of the book: *Boris Johnson – The
Blond Beast of Brexit – A Study in Depravity.*

Is this poetry? Williams' style is
hard to pin down. He called his poems
investigations: reportage with the

tones and textures of prose but with the facts
marshalled in a way that is undeniably
poetic. Polemic is a word that

has been used to describe the writing, as
has satirical, radical, argumentative.
Williams is often compared to

Jonathan Swift. He gives us satire
aimed at power: presidents, politicians,
monarchs, corporations, and empire.

The Blond Beast of Brexit veers more on
the side of tract rather than poem. It
is on the prosaic side of the Williams'

spectrum. Elsewhere, however, Williams takes
the factual bones of social critique and
arranges them into beautiful sculptures:

his *Whale Nation, Sacred Elephant,*
and *Autogeddon* are majestic litanies
and laments.

2.

They have solid building blocks. Facts are laid
out in a way that makes them sing, incite, and awe.
Whale Nation tells us about that animal. It starts:

From space, the planet is blue.
From space, the planet is the territory
Not of humans, but of the whale.

Facts are listed then analysed. Associations
spring from the materials, while being
woven from a subjective point of view. We

leap, as we might from premise to conclusion,
into a poetic sublime. Facts become
magic. *Sacred Elephant*, another

"investigative" poem, works similar
miracles. At one point, it compares an
Indian elephant's ear with the shape of

India, an African elephant's ear
with Africa – comparisons that seem
more than fitting, more than coincidental

in Williams' careful hands. There is menace,
too, in the descriptions of human avarice,
ignorance and perversion. *Autogeddon*

is a poem that makes a counter-intuitive
argument. It claims the motorcar represents
an "undeclared war": its global death toll,

its emissions, its reliance on oil –
all manifestations of the corrupt
decadence of humanity, of our

unbridled, self-destructive impulses.
Whether you agree or not you are mesmerized
as Williams mines fact after fact – the same

way corporations mine oil, plumbing ancient
depths for Earth's life blood, the liquefied
transmutation of life itself.

3.

Sometime in the year 1933, in
Trinidad and Tobago, Michael de Freitas
was born. In 1957 he migrated

to the colonial motherland.
In England, by the 1960s, he
renamed himself "Michael X", became

a black power activist. He helped organise
the first outdoor Notting Hill Carnival.
But soon the carnival was over. He

fell afoul of the law, was accused
of race offences, extortion. He
fled to Trinidad in 1971.

He formed a commune. It burned down. Police
investigating the fire found two
bodies. He was convicted of murdering

one and, because Trinidad still had capital
punishment, he was hanged. Trinidad was
not yet a republic: the Queen had to

sign the death warrant. The hanging took place
in what is called The Royal Jail on
Frederick Street, Port of Spain. There is a

story that claims Heathcote Williams sprayed
graffiti on the walls of Buckingham
Palace in protest against the Queen signing

Michael X's death warrant. For Williams,
protest, satire, separating the
wheat from chaff – that is the stuff of poetry.

"If poetry isn't revolutionary,
it's nothing," he said. "Poetry is
heightened language, and language exists to

effect change, not to be a tranquilliser."
So even his most pedestrian tracts
have the essence of verse. They are like

the graffiti that appears overnight
bridging darkness and light.

4.

What is graffiti if not visual poetry?
We should regard Williams' poetry as words
scrawled on the walls of the palace.

5.

Answer this: Why must poetry be limited
to the lyrical? Free verse, prose poems,
concrete poems, sonic poems, film

poems, procedural poems – the poem
is not a closed category. It can
accommodate a wide range of textures,

it can come in a wide range of forms.
To the ancient Greeks, anything *lyrikos*
was anything good enough for the lyre.

To the English in the 1500s, it
was anything of strong emotion or
things meant to be sung. Later it became

anything musical, the words of a song.
The word lyrical itself is an archive
suggesting poetry's hybrid forms. The

essay, with its act of weighing, with its
forward propulsion, its persuasive
endeavour, can itself be lyric. As

Alice Notley's *The Descent of Allette*
reminds us, entire novels can be
written in verse. So too can essays.

In a sense, Williams was writing essays.
But that does not mean he was not writing
poetry.

THE FREE COLONY

To plunder, to slaughter, to steal, these things they misname empire; and where they make a wilderness, they call it peace.

— Tacitus

I. From Columbus to Brexit

When Christopher Columbus set foot on the island he called San Salvador in 1492, he stowed us on a vessel whose destination is yet to be fully reached. Our voyage came to a halt some time ago when as colonial subjects we wrongly mistook independence for freedom, when our colonial master successfully triggered a break-up of the relationship. Like a manipulative boyfriend who wants out, but does not want to be the one to actually do it, the master created the conditions that would push his lover away – by behaving badly and planting the false idea that there was an uncrossable ocean of difference between himself and us, his subject. When the subject at last asked for an end to the affair, the master happily complied.

Motivating the so-called independence movement of the 1960s and the granting of independence was not the idea of freedom, but of race. Colonial subjects were citizens of the British Empire. They could (and I will argue should) have been fully integrated into Great Britain and given the right to name Her Majesty's prime minister at the polls. But the idea of black, brown, or yellow bodies from overseas taking root at Westminster; the idea of a society in which a pale class is no longer wholly in control of power had to be avoided at all costs, as remains the case today in Britain, with the fear of the foreign, of the fear, for instance, of Turkey joining the European Union.

As the campaign and vote for Brexit has shown, exclusive nationalism and racial hatred are the most powerful of human impulses. They are more powerful than reason, more powerful than economics, more powerful than any system of political belief, more powerful than faith in a god, more powerful than art and literature. It was racism that shaped the world during the 1950s and 1960s, ensuring that the empire on which the sun never set did not become a beacon of light. It was a Labour minister of state who wanted to turn the *Empire Windrush* back to the Caribbean in 1948. If the colonies had not been granted independence, if instead they had been granted true equality within the Empire, I believe we would be much closer to the destination towards which we set sail in 1492: a multicultural world in which, at last, the humanity that resides in all of us is acknowledged. But of course the subjunctive world of "would" is an easier world to live in than the historic tense of reality.

So the colonies were given a flimsy independence built on precarious internal social divides between haves and have-nots, and amid severe economic imbalances between the centre and the periphery. In short, the new nations were left to form ghettos of their own. Decades later, the problems of these jilted countries – I speak of the broader ex-colonial world, American, Belgian, British, Dutch, French, Portuguese and Spanish – now imperil the welfare of the same former colonial masters. Both Europe and North America face unprecedented threats of terror due to resentful extremism; economic vulnerabilities at the hands of rising Chinese power; a wrong-headed refusal to accept the limitations climate change now demands, and the spread of all sorts of contagion because poorer nations are less able to afford the prophylactic defences available to their bigger sisters and brothers.

The lesson we have learned is this: be careful what you wish for.

In the past, I have been anxious about the re-emergence of calls for decolonisation. I have feared these calls repeated the same mistake of the past. I have worried that in calling for things to be dismantled, the decolonising mission has suggested the possibility of estrangement – a re-enforcing of the impossible idea of separateness.

But my worries ignored the fact that this discourse has re-emerged half a century after the independence movement. The fact that after so much time we are still calling for a re-envisioning of the world is an admission that political independence was but one step in a larger process that remains outstanding. The calls for the abandonment of archaic laws, outmoded systems, covert influence, and oppressive power structures seek not only to dismantle, they also seek to build and bridge. As Félix Patzi Paco has argued, "decolonisation … struggles against all types of racism and reclaims the inalienable principle that we are all equal".[1]

What is needed now is an admission that we live in a diverse, multinational society which needs to reflect our shared humanity; that we live in a complex world in which every creed and race needs to find an equal place – a world shorn of economic, technological, and even artistic privileges premised on racial superiority. By this I do not necessarily mean a concept

---

1. See Félix Patzi Paco, "Decolonisation", translated by Yoán Moreno, *The Miami Rail*, Winter, 2016. Given the length of this essay, references are provided as footnotes in the body of the text.

of a "third space" or "positionality" as put forward by Homi Bhabha and Stuart Hall.[2] Nor am I exhorting, as the titular character does in Stephen Cobham's 1907 novel *Rupert Gray*, a rose-tinted idea of imperialism being perfected through the "exclusion of inequality among the races".[3] Imperialism, with its hierarchy involving monarch or emperor, is inherently bound up with inequality, both internally in relation to the leader and in terms of how the empire envisions itself when positioned against competing nations. No, true equality would mean the end of the imperial agenda. It would mean freezing the map: not seeking to annex new states, nor recklessly seeking to off-load colonies, but instead acknowledging that the relationship has been unequal and unjust, and consolidating rights and privileges hitherto denied.

★

The world likes to forget it, but millions of colonial subjects fought in wars on the empire's behalf. Colonials such as Trinidad's Captain Arthur Cipriani, lobbied for the chance to fight in World War One:

> West Indians have realized it is a fight to the finish, that not only is the existence of the Mother Country at stake, but the very Empire of which we are all proud to be a part. We should feel not only isolated but slighted if our services are declined when men are still wanted to keep the flag flying.[4]

Though Cipriani saw a comity of peoples united under empire; the British West Indian contingent was subject to discrimination and neglect. After the war, Sir Algernon E. Aspinall (1871-1952), chairman of the West Indian committee, noted, "It is really deplorable that so little interest should have been taken in the British West Indian Contingent"[5].

During the Second World War, 1,440,500 soldiers hailed from India, 629,000 were Canadians, 413,000 came from Australia, 136,000 came from South Africa, 128,500 from New Zealand and more than 134,000 travelled from other colonies, including some 10,000 from the Caribbean. The treatment of demobbed black soldiers was no better. Many who settled in Britain after the war as empire citizens struggled in a climate of racist hostility. Allan Wilmot, a Jamaican who had volunteered to join the Royal Navy, recalled life after service, saying, "Being British you feel like you are coming home but when we came here it was like we dropped out of the sky.

2. As referenced by Jak Peake, *Between the Bocas* (Liverpool: Liverpool University Press, 2017), p. 30.
3. *Rupert Gray: A Study in Black and White* (Mona: UWI Press, 2006), p.
4 See C.L.R. James, *The Life of Captain Cipriani* (Durham: Duke University Press, 2014), p. 65.
5. *The Life of Captain Cipriani*, p. 65

Nobody knew anything about us."[6] Many black ex-servicemen (and black women) helped to rebuild postwar Britain, changing its landscape forever, just as their enslaved ancestors had, by the efforts of their commoditised bodies, added to the wealth of the colonial motherland. Yet still, the mother could not accept her progeny. Why? It was all too evidently because of race.

What happened after the WWII and in the "independence" decade of the 1960s was a continuation of the wrongs perpetrated by the colonial master: the violent eradication of indigenous populations in the name of God and gold; the enslavement of millions of Africans; the trafficking of indentured labourers from India and China to replace freed slaves; the use of military might to subjugate entire societies while reaping their wealth. To do this the colonial master had to deny the humanity of the colonised races. As Aimé Césaire declared: "Between coloniser and colonized there is room only for forced labour, intimidation, pressure, the police, taxation, theft, rape, compulsory crops, contempt, mistrust, arrogance, self-complacency, swinishness, brainless elites, degraded masses."[7] The colonial master claimed to act in the name of god and civilisation, but had merely succeeded in grafting "modern abuse onto ancient injustice, hateful racism onto old inequality".[8]

But Césaire's conclusion that the colonised should follow nationalist independence policies in Africa, the South Sea Islands, Madagascar and the West Indies and his call for a revolution has to be questioned. What should have been the priority was equality, not independence. What was needed was integration that had human dignity at its heart. The empire should have been made to expand and to absorb, as the heart expands, over time, when exercised by the body's limbs. A deeper, more genuine union, premised on equal rights in all areas of life, should have been the centre of a multicultural ferment in a space where the intoxicating mixture of races and cultures could have enhanced world society. What would have been so strange about the idea of the descendants of slaves still in the islands standing at Westminster? What was so unfathomable about the idea of the descendants of coolies standing in the same premises as their former masters? There was only one thing that prevented all of this: race. The basis of that new social order would have been what colonisation had sought to erase: the fact that there was never any real difference between the coloniser and the colonised. Beneath the skin of each, the same colour blood flowed in their veins, both had divine rights by virtue of their humanity, both had rich and varied histories, cultures, societies, and political systems. Both colonised and

---

6. See the BBC report 'Soldiers of the Caribbean: Britain's forgotten war heroes' http://www.bbc.com/news/uk-32703753
7. Aimé Césaire, *Discourse on Colonialism* (New York: Monthly Review Press, 2000), p. 42.
8. Ibid, p. 45.

coloniser lived in societies that were rife with conflict and contradictions of, for instance, ethnicity and class. Of Prospero, George Lamming appropriately remarked, "his encounter with Caliban is, largely, his encounter with himself."[9] Even Césaire sensed this when he wrote:

> I admit that it is a good thing to place different civilisations in contact with each other; that it is an excellent thing to blend different worlds; that whatever its own particular genius may be, a civilisation that withdraws into itself atrophies; that for civilisations, exchange is oxygen; that the great good fortune of Europe is to have been a crossroads, and that because it was the locus of all ideas, the receptacle of all philosophies, the meeting place of all sentiments, it was the best centre for the redistribution of energy.[10]

But a limited notion of decolonisation would perpetuate a superficial freedom: a false view of a dichotomy between the coloniser and colonised; what Frantz Fanon called, "a world compartmentalised, Manichaean and petrified".[11] In other words, you against me, friend versus enemy, Carl Schmidt's other.[12]

Yet, Fanon, too, was guilty of the same Manichaeism he criticised when he called on colonised people who had migrated to the metropolis "to change sides" and to "leave… Europe".[13] It should have been the destiny of colonial subjects to have been acknowledged as an equal part of the new amalgam history had formed. Instead of being urged to leave Europe, the colonised should have been encouraged to become integral to it through the granting of full representation. For, as we shall see, it was an error to think that, once separated, both parties could live happily every after without one another. It was wrong of Fanon to assert that "independence is…an indispensable condition for men and women to exist in true liberation… to master all the material resources necessary for a radical transformation of society".[14] In truth, it was the opposite.

But doesn't my argument suffer from a rosy-tinted naïveté? Can the colonial subject really be faulted for aspiring to something that appeared more immediately achievable than the kind of post-imperial integration I've been arguing? For would the former master ever willingly admit that he was no different from those he once ruled over? To accept the colonial

---

9. George Lamming, *The Pleasures of Exile* (London: Michael Joseph, 1960), p. 15.
10. *Discourse on Colonialism*, p. 33.
11. *The Wretched of the Earth* (New York: Grove Press, 2004), p. 15.
12. Carl Schmitt, *The Concept of the Political*, translated by George Schwab (Chicago: University of Chicago Press, 1996), pp. 26-27.
13. *The Wretched of the Earth* (New York: Grove Press, 2004), p. 235.
14. Ibid., p. 233.

population as being part of the national identity of the motherland would be to admit there was no difference between a white man and a black man. It would mean knowing that those on the beach at Dunkirk were not only persons from the British Isles, but also from the entire empire. But as Christopher Nolan's film *Dunkirk* (2017) demonstrates – it erased entirely the role played by black and brown colonials – that idea is still evidently difficult for many to swallow.

★

Independence in the 1960s had the outward semblance of inevitability. In truth, it was the least appropriate option on the table. Centuries earlier, in the 1760s and 1770s, a debate raged on both sides of the Atlantic over the future shape of the Empire. It was believed by colonists in North America that they deserved the right to have a say in the British parliament. If they were to be taxed, surely they were equal to any other citizen of Britain?

Britain had grown in power, wealth and influence from the revenues drawn from its colonial economies. Towards the end of the seventeenth century, the British parliament began to promulgate laws regulating imperial commerce. By the mid 18th century the colonies were generating such private wealth that the British state wanted a share. In 1765, parliament imposed a tax on the colonies, the so-called Stamp Act. This was a direct tax on a variety of colonial goods, including all materials printed in the colonies. The tax faced strong opposition in the North American colonies. Parliament balked, repealing it. But it still wanted to assert its authority to do as it pleased to its colonial subjects, even though they had no voting rights at Westminster. In the 1766 Declaratory Act, British MPs proclaimed they "had, hath and of rights ought to have, full power and authority to make laws and statutes of sufficient force and validity to bind the colonies and people of America…in all cases whatsoever." One MP helpfully explained that parliament, "represents the whole British Empire, and (therefore) has authority to bind every part and every subject without the least distinction, whether such subjects have a right to vote or not, or whether the law binds places within the realm or without."[15] Of course, at this time, only around 3% of the British population had the vote.

This was part of a continuing trend of brazenness on the part of the master. In the eighteenth century, the British parliament regulated the colonial money supply, the development of colonial manufacturing, and the imposition of taxes. In 1764, customs duties on colonial imports were levied, and restrictions on colonial trade with the French West Indies

15. Charles A. Kromkowski, *Recreating the American Republic: Rules of Apportionment, Constitutional Change, and American Political Development, 1700–1870* (Cambridge: Cambridge University Press, 2002), p.117.

introduced.[16] The 1764 Sugar Act was designed to generate revenue for the British Treasury. By 1768, parliament imposed another set of customs duties on colonial imports. These revenues were used to fund the very system of colonial subjugation: paying the salaries of royal governors and judges. There were more protests, including an American boycott of British imports, as well as violent disturbances in several colonial cities. Once more, British MPs retreated, but only up to a point. They rescinded the duties on everything except imported tea. So with every sip of that ubiquitous drink American colonials had to swallow British dominance. Far from being chastened as to the limits of their powers, "members of Parliament and most of the British political elite continued to envision British-colonial relations in terms of the latter subordinated to the former."[17]

In response to the 1764 Sugar Act, James Otis of Massachusetts had argued that "no parts of His Majesty's dominions can be taxed without their consent" and that "every part" of the British Empire, "has a right to be represented in the supreme or some subordinate legislature":

> That the colonists, black and white, born here, are freeborn British subjects, and entitled to all the essential civil rights of such, is a truth not only manifest from the provincial charters, from the principles of the common law, and acts of parliament; but from the British constitution, which was re-established at the revolution, with a professed design to lecture the liberties of all the subjects to all generations.[18]

Otis proposed allocating colonial representation in the British parliament in "some proportion to their number and estates". This extension of parliamentary representation, he said, would integrate both sides of the Atlantic, giving "both countries a thorough knowledge of each others interests". For him, "this would firmly unite all parts of the British empire, in the greatest peace and prosperity; and render it invulnerable and perpetual."[19]

Otis was not alone. Richard Stockton of New Jersey recommended that each colony, "send one or two of their most ingenious fellows" to the British House of Commons and "maintain them there till they can maintain themselves, or else we shall be fleeced to some purpose"[20]. Like Otis, Joseph Galloway of Pennsylvania saw benefits accruing to both sides. Galloway believed colonial representatives would provide "a new door of

---

16. Ibid, p.117.
17. Ibid, p. 118.
18. James Otis, 'The Rights of the British Colonies Asserted and Proved', 1763 – http://oll.libertyfund.org/pages/1763-otis-rights-of-british-colonies-asserted-pamphlet
19. Kromkowski, p. 124.

Information" on colonial affairs for British legislators, and he felt colonials would "conceive it their Duty to obey Institutions and Laws agreed on by their own representatives". This would add a newfound cohesiveness to the empire as it would "form the Strongest and most indissoluble Bond of Union, that can be invented, between the mother Country and her Foreign Dominions".[21] Governor Bernard of Massachusetts had more pragmatic reasons for backing the idea. He privately suggested that "30 (seats in parliament) for the Continent & 15 for the Islands [the British Caribbean] would be sufficient"[22] to give the colonists enough representation so as to win obedience to parliament. For similar reasons, former Quebec Attorney General Francis Maseres recommended in 1770 the addition of eighty new members from the North American and Caribbean colonies.[23]

Even before the breakdown in relations between the American colonies and Britain, the idea that it was only proper for colonists to be represented at Westminster was circulating in the Caribbean. In 1651, the Barbados Assembly asked:

> Shall we be bound to the Government and Lordship of a Parliament in which we have no Representatives, or persons chosen by us, for there to propound and consent to what might be needful to us, as also to oppose and dispute all what should tend to our disadvantage and harm? In truth, this would be a slavery far exceeding all that the English nation hath yet suffered.[24]

In 1689, Barbadian planter Edward Littleton wrote a pamphlet in which he noted a colonial desire for parliamentary representation. Littleton complained that, "our Masters…think they have a great advantage over us" because "we have none to represent us in Parliament".[25]

At this stage, representation in Parliament was definitely a favoured alternative to independence. At this stage, views on both sides of the Atlantic were shaped by feelings of common race and kinship. In 1770, Virginian George Mason said, "there are not five Men of Sense in America who wou'd accept of Independence if it was offered." In October 1774, George Washington declared, "that no such thing is desired by any thinking man in all North America; on the contrary, that is the ardent wish of the warmest advocates for liberty, that peace & tranquillity, upon constitutional grounds, may be restored, & the horrors of civil discord prevented".

---

20. Ibid, p. 125.
21. Kromkowski, p. 125.
22. Ibid, p. 125.
23. Ibid, p. 126.
24. *Declaration of the Barbados Assembly*, Feb. 18, 1651.
24. Kromkowski, p. 124
25. Ibid, p. 122.

Two years later, in 1776, the idea remained so abhorrent that John Adams of Massachusetts observed, "Independency is an Hobgoblin, of so frightful Mein, that it would throw a delicate Person into Fits to look it in the face."[26] What also lay behind the 18th century preference for representation over independence was the particular hobgoblin of race. Particularly in the Caribbean colonies – and no doubt in some of the North American colonies with significant enslaved populations – fears of black insurrection were very real. In the Caribbean islands, Blacks outnumbered Whites by as much as 10-1. These were powerful reasons to remain under the imperial wing and its military might.

There were a few positive responses from the British to the demand for representation. In 1775, one plan was published in London that coupled a proposal for reconciling the British-colonial conflict with another for making representation "equal over all Great Britain, in proportion to the number of Inhabitants".[27] A year later, British pamphleteer Joshua Steel recommended for the "union and utility of the whole, a new sovereign council, consisting of deputies from each province of the Great Commonwealth".[28]

The idea received much, but mostly negative attention in the British press. Steele admitted in 1766 that the idea, "would go so much against the stomachs of some of our countrymen, that it could never be got down; nay would disgust them to that degree, that I think they would not suffer any plan to be brought before them that savoured of such a doctrine". As legal historian John Phillip Reid recounts, various objections were raised. It was feared the colonial representatives would become, "a party, a faction, a flying squadron" that would serve to "distress government". One opponent feared, ironically, that the House of Commons would be taken over by a powerful faction that would, "overset the throne" or "enslave the people". In 1769, Edmund Burke dismissed the proposal speculating that "the author had dropped down from the moon, without any knowledge of the general nature of this globe, of the general nature of its inhabitants, without the least acquaintance with the affairs of this country". He raised, too, the more pragmatic problems with the idea of colonial representation, such as the burden of the expenses, including trans-Atlantic transportation of these new parliamentary members as well as the "infinite difficulty of settling that representation on a fair balance of wealth and numbers". Isaac Barre argued against the idea using more blunt considerations. For him, the colonies, "will grow more numerous than we are and then how inconvenient and dangerous would it be to have representatives of 7 millions there meet the representatives of 7 millions here". It was safer to have half the population disenfranchised.[29]

---

26. Ibid, p. 128
27. Ibid, p. 128.
28. Ibid, p. 127

It was only with the American Revolution that the debate ended. Not willing to grant colonists the status they called for, Britain paid the price as America ceded from the Empire. Even so, the lesson was not learned. Outside of America, taxation without representation lasted well into the 20th century for the remaining colonies. For example, in St. Lucia there were export duties on bay leaves, bay oil, charcoal, cocoa, coconut oil, coconuts, copra, firewood, hard wood, lime products, log wood, molasses and syrup, pimento wood, sugar, whale oil and fish oils. In St. Christopher and Nevis cotton and coconuts were taxed; in Jamaica, spirits. In Trinidad, asphalt was subject to export duties.[30]

When the independence movements began in earnest, it could not be said the master was unaware of what should have been the first and, I believe, most desirable option: granting all its peoples full franchise. Instead, in place of Colonial Office and white minority dominated Crown Colony constitutions, it established shambolic "advisory" councils in which, whilst there was universal suffrage, the elected representatives had no power; these councils were merely rehearsals for supposedly autonomous and independent parliaments. Here, of course, the dialogue was thwarted by imperial contempt for those subject peoples of African and Indian origins. When one of those colonial quasi-governments dared to challenge the colonial order, as the elected government in British Guiana did in 1953, over the matter of trade union representation, the British Government sent in troops, suspended the constitution and imprisoned leading politicians.[31]

Granting Independence under the conditions in which it was offered represented moral failure upon moral failure. It was essentially the final act of the British abandonment of the Caribbean and its peoples that began with an emancipation process that rewarded the slave-owners and made no reparation to the formerly enslaved – all part of the dwindling importance of Caribbean sugar to British interests. What should have been granted was a right to universal representation on an equal basis and forms of devolution with respect to local matters. The failure to grant this paved the way for a parting of ways. Otis had dreamt that, "The next universal monarchy will be favourable to the human race... founded on the principles of equity, moderation and justice." Instead, the next universal order was founded on ideas of segregation, race and covert economic dominance.

★

29. Ibid, p. 129
30. *Hansard,* HC Deb 24 February 1932 vol 262 cc368-71 [Electronic version].
31. For a participant account see Cheddi Jagan, *The West On Trial* (London: Michael Joseph, 1966); for a poetic crystallisation of those days see Martin Carter's *Poems of Resistance from British Guiana* (London: Lawrence & Wishart, 1954)

Two debates that took place decades before the 1960s give insight into the race-thinking that would later play an important role in the motivations of both sides in the drive towards political independence. These debates involved the separate but similar ideas of the Caribbean being annexed to the United States of America or to Canada.

In many respects, the Caribbean and North America are natural bedfellows. They are near neighbours, and both have cause to commiserate having histories involving colonial rule. For the Caribbean, union would fuse small islands to vastly larger economies. And, as Harvey R. Neptune tells it, the US wartime occupation of Trinidad in the 1940s not only broke rigid colonial hierarchies, with white US soldiers "secreting intimacies across the colour line", but injected a new dynamism into the Trinidadian economy and gave many African and Indian workers new ideas about themselves.[32] And yet, while America presented the prospect of a different kind of liberation, removing the conventions and strictures of British colonialist attitudes, the thought of annexation to the USA was coloured by fears that in truth the change would be a case of jumping out of the frying pan and into the racial fire. Such fears, as Neptune notes, were recorded in the book-length essay, *Confederation of the British West Indies versus Annexation to the United States of America: A Political Discourse on the West Indies.* Written by Dr. Louis Meikle and appearing in 1912, Meikle argued against annexation, placing emphasis on the problem of white supremacist attitudes in the US, citing the current spate of lynchings in particular. Meikle argued that US whites would, unlike their British comparators who ruled from afar, be in direct competition with black people because of their closer proximity. Meikle summed it up bluntly: "The West Indian, as a negro, is not wanted in the United States of America, which is the home of fifteen million of his race."[33]

This concern deepened a pre-existing prejudice against US culture that came from British rule. As George Lamming observed in *The Pleasures of Exile,* for the West Indian, "a foreign or absent Mother culture has always cradled his judgement",[34] making him see the world in terms of myths which idealised Britain and denigrated competing claims for supremacy represented by the US:

> This myth begins in the West Indian from the earliest stages of his education. But it is not yet turned against America. In a sense, America does not even exist. It begins with the fact of England's supremacy in taste and judgment: a fact which can only have meaning and weight by a calculated

32. Harvey R. Neptune, *Caliban and the Yankees* (Chapel Hill: The University of North Carolina Press, 2007), p. 60.
33. Louis Meikle, Confederation of the British West Indies versus Annexation to the United States of America: A Political Discourse on the West Indies, London: Sampson Low, Marston & Company Ltd, 1912, p. 7.

cutting down to size of all non-England. The first to be cut down is the colonial himself. [35]

Anxiety over race and ambivalence on the part of the colonial subject in relation to North America was understandable. Having been subject to slavery, indentureship, and then a bruising second-class citizenship, it is not hard to see why there was a fear that new, untested alliances risked simply exchanging one master for another.

On the part of the colonising forces, race thinking was equally influential – and deeply perverse. Having built and consolidated empires with the ostensible aim of civilising the non-white races, fear of racial variety itself was then used to spurn full union.

This dynamic was apparent when it came to the idea of a union between Canada and the Caribbean. According to Brinsley Samaroo, for a lot of Caribbean colonials, the grass appeared greener on the Canadian side. In 1884, two attempts were made to raise the matter with Canada. One came from absentee Jamaican and Leeward Island planters, another came from Barbados. It seems clear these efforts were motivated by pique given the British government's failure to impose countervailing duties against bounty-fed European sugar. Nothing came of these approaches.

But in 1911 the matter resurfaced, the Bahamas Legislature asked imperial government to begin negotiations. The Colonial Office said no, citing the racial differences between the two groups of people, differences which it said could raise problems.[36] Still, the matter would not die. In 1918, it arose again and one letter-writer, a Canadian businessman with Caribbean ties, wrote in a newspaper: "Canadians, it is felt, would object to black and coloured populations being admitted to federations on terms of equality with themselves, and would not relish such men sitting in the Canadian parliament."[37] Such a statement makes plain the main obstacle to true political union.

This obstacle finds even clearer expression in the experience of the French Union. In a review of European colonial regimes, A.W. Brian Simpson notes the dramatic disconnect between what France set out on paper in relation to its empire and the reality of the relationship. On the one hand the constitution of 1946 stated:

France forms with the people of its overseas territories a Union based upon equality of rights and duties without distinction of race or religion...

---

34. *The Pleasures of Exile,* p.35.
35. Ibid, p. 27.
36. Brinsley Samaroo, "The Politics of Disharmony: The Debate on the Political. Union of the British West Indies & Canada, 1884-1921," *Revista Interamericana,* Vol. VII, No. 1 (Spring 1977), p. 53.
37. Ibid, p. 57.

> The French Union is composed of nations and peoples who wish to place in common or coordinate their resources, and their efforts, in order to develop their civilisation, increase their wellbeing and ensure their security.[38]

However, France would still be the boss: "Faithful to her traditional mission, France proposes to guide the peoples for whom she has assumed responsibility toward freedom to govern themselves and democratically to manage their own affairs." The proposal was never debated, but was rather a *fait accompli*. Democratic management of autonomous affairs was trumped by French "responsibility". The 1946 constitution provided no legal mechanisms to give force to the supposed equality enjoyed by all. Its declaration of rights was not backed up by enforceable remedies or systems of judicial review. While in theory there were no French colonies, just a French Union, or just one France, legislative power was vested in Paris. A grand assembly of the Union had merely consultative weight. Simpson observes, "the colonies participated in the legislative process, though only to a limited extent."[39] In sum:

> Representation was not in any way proportional to population, and the elaborate electoral systems were not based upon universal suffrage, even though citizenship was in theory universal; in reality universal citizenship was something of a fiction. Local assemblies did exist, but they had very limited power and influence, for example over the structure of local budgets.[40]

It is difficult to separate the ambivalence of the French approach to its Union from social considerations. The atrocities of the Algerian War and the Paris massacre of 1961, denied and censored by French society for decades, only seem possible in the context of a system of collective political action and belief in which the notion of equality had been distorted by agendas of race and creed; by discrimination, whether unconscious or conscious, designed to be masked by a veneer of *liberté, égalité, fraternité*.

James Otis, of course, could not have predicted all this. But some might have guessed at the difficulties ahead given the situation in the US itself where, upon independence, founding fathers famously declared "that all men are created equal" while, for some, these self-evident rights did not extend to enslaved black bodies. Indeed, when the US eventually held its own colonies (in reality if not in name), contradictions revolving around race played out in the marginalisation of these territories – such as Cuba,

---

38. Quoted in A.W. Brian Simpson, *Human Rights and the End of Empire* (Oxford: Oxford University Press, 2004), p. 285.
39. Ibid, p. 286.
40. Ibid, p. 286.

Haiti, the Philippines, Puerto Rico, and the US Virgin islands – and their removal from the idea of America itself. As Daniel Immerwahr wrote:

> The racism that had pervaded the country since slavery also engulfed the territories. Like African Americans, colonial subjects were denied the vote, deprived of the rights of full citizens, called racial epithets, subjected to dangerous medical experiments and used as sacrificial pawns in war. They, too, had to make their way in a country where some lives mattered and others did not.[40]

★

One day after France's Charles de Gaulle recognized the independence of Algeria, British MPs met at Westminster on July 4, 1962. The task at hand was the granting of independence to a new country, Trinidad and Tobago. With hearty congratulations, Her Majesty's MPs commended the Trinidad and Tobago Independence Bill. But every single MP who spoke during the debate saw that the new country would be born with crippling birth defects. Like many other former colonies, it would be a country built on a society riddled with inter-ethnic strife – some of which had served the interests of the colonialists by dividing and conquering. It would also be a society left at the mercy of mercantile forces still centred in the metropolitan world. The imperial master knew that independence would solve nothing, yet saw bright prospects ahead in the extraction of natural resources (oil and natural gas) that required the context of an apparently independent but in reality still dependent nation. That neo-colonial nation came into existence in 1962. And, as a result, a fully functioning, economically sovereign nation still does not exist today.

Reginald Maudling, the secretary of state for the colonies, spoke glowingly of the new country's strengths. "There is the famous pitch lake which provides so much of the world's road surfaces," he said, "and perhaps I should not fail to mention the other products in which Trinidad has a world monopoly, Angostura bitters." Perhaps these formidable resources made up for the country's race problem, which even the enthusiastic Maudling was forced to admit:

> I must say frankly that when I visited Trinidad earlier this year... I was very much aware of the possible development of racial tensions within the island [...] Politics in the island were polarised between the Government party largely supported by people of African background, and the opposition party largely supported by people of Indian background. That, to my mind, was a very real danger.[42]

---

41. Daniel Immerwahr, "How the US has hidden its empire", *Guardian*, February 15, 2019.

This recognition took place in the context of the beginnings of a racial war that broke out in February 1962 between Africans and Indians in British Guiana – a war that claimed nearly 200 lives between 1962-1964. Notwithstanding this "very real danger", Maudling took comfort in the country's constitution which, he said, contained, "considerable safeguards for minorities and individuals". He gave the country this mandate: "the people of Trinidad and Tobago will have a special responsibility in the years ahead to prove what can be done in a relatively small island with a very mixed people". Never mind what could have been done in the British Isles, or that racial diversity was often cited as a reason to deny integrative movements elsewhere.

Decades later, Trinidad and Tobago's politics remains beset by racial animosity between these two ethnic groups. The problems of governance and development have been hindered by a token democracy that rewards racial allegiance and not performance. The country's considerable natural resources exist within an economy dominated by outside forces. As a result, governments come and go with impunity while the country's murder rate has spiralled to one of the highest in the world. Trinidad and Tobago also has the highest per capita rate of ISIS recruitment in the western hemi-sphere,[43] a troubling statistic in a world which has seen Islamic terrorists attack the precincts of Westminster.

No one can see the future, but on July 4, 1962, MPs saw enough to know there were storm clouds ahead. "The Secretary of State for the Colonies has given an optimistic picture of the economic possibilities of these two islands as an independent country," said John Strachey, the Dundee West MP, "but we must recognise that they face very great complications and difficulties in doing so, and we must still be intimately concerned to help them." Oil reserves were a blessing and a curse. Long before successive prime ministers of Trinidad and Tobago had to tackle sudden recessions due to declining oil prices, Strachey foresaw the topsy-turvey economy that was being formed.

"The future of these communities in the Caribbean and many others in the Middle East, both inside and outside the Commonwealth, is bound up with the outlook in the world oil trade, and when that trade is dominated by a handful of great international corporations," said Strachey. "They have now become so vast that they dominate the economic future prospects of communities such as Trinidad and Tobago." He continued, "Upon this country becoming independent, we have the creation of another independ-

---

42. For this and all the following quotations of speeches from this debate, see *Hansard*, HC Deb 04 July 1962 vol 662 cc541-75.
43. US Department of State: Country Reports on Terrorism 2016 https://www.state.gov/reports/country-reports-on-terrorism-2016/

ent oil State, whose whole future is deeply bound up with the vast, worldwide question of the conduct of the oil industry". He explained that the "gigantic enterprise of oil" was "different from any other commercial enterprise in the world, and is entirely in the hands of a great oligopoly – to use the economists' term – of oil companies, with their peculiar pricing policy."

And how could any real action be taken to reform the structure of the economy if all the island's inhabitants were preoccupied with fending off attacks from each other? Nigel Fisher, the Surbiton MP, saw, "racial difficulties between those of African and Indian descent." He added, "politically, from now on it is up to Trinidad herself. If she can resolve her own racial problem, which is the most difficult of all, I am sure that she will have a hopeful and happy future." Yet what country of the world has been able to resolve its "racial problem"? Instead of transforming the empire, with its long history of strong institutions, to become a beacon of multiculturalism by granting voting rights to its diverse peoples, that task was left to a twin-island republic of 800,000 inhabitants. Said Fisher:

> Given good will and understanding, I am sure that she can do that. It will require tolerance and statesmanship from the leaders of both races. I want Trinidad to prove that she possesses these qualities, as I am sure she does. I want her to set an example to other nations, larger nations, faced with this same problem. We are all gratified that she is staying within the British Commonwealth of Nations and that she will continue to owe allegiance to the Crown.

But concerning the new constitution, which was supposedly the solution to the racial problem, Joan Vickers, Plymouth Devonport MP, was not entirely convinced:

> When I was in Trinidad and read the draft Constitution I found that there were thirty or forty instances of power being vested in the hands of the Prime Minister of the day. It is still felt that there are too few members of the minority races in the police, in judicial posts in the Civil Service and the Army. I hope that, in future, due opportunity will be given to all races to serve in those posts if they so wish.

Upon making this point, she was quickly interrupted by Fisher:

> I am sorry to interrupt my Hon. Friend, but I know that she appreciates that there is no racial difficulty about this at all. In the police, the Army, and so on, it is simply a matter of attaining certain physical standards, in rather the same way as in this country. That is the main limiting factor. I do not think that anyone has been excluded from public service on grounds of race.

Miss Vickers returned:

I thank my Hon. Friend, but that is what I have heard. I think it rather astonishing that there should be such a considerable number of those descended from Negro, African and not of other stocks who are considered to be physically and educationally fit. That should be watched very carefully, because I cannot see why those of one race should be so predominantly better physically than the others, when all have been brought up in equal surroundings. Perhaps, as I say, some of these people have not been so keen on joining but, with independence, they are now more eager.

Five decades later, Nizam Mohammed, the chairman of Trinidad and Tobago's police service commission was fired after he questioned what he described as a racial imbalance of officers within the same police service and along the same terms. Six years after this, Dr Keith Rowley, the prime minister, would publicly deny claims the same police service was targeting East Indian politicians. The perception of imbalance Vickers saw in 1962 seems to have lingered.

Though every MP recognized the politics of the place was split on the basis of race, they proceeded to praise Trinidad and Tobago's prime minister, Dr Eric Williams. He was from the ruling PNM party, a party which the MPs acknowledged was aligned to persons of African descent. Williams was mentioned 37 times in the debate – mostly in glowing tribute – while the East Indian opposition leader, Dr Rudranath Capildeo, was mentioned four times by name. The very debate was a political coup for the ruling party and itself perpetuated the ethnic tension the MPs spoke of. "There are bound to be differences of opinion," Eirene White, the Flint East MP, said of the race issue before adding:

I heard Dr. Williams' broadcast on the subject of the Constitution. It was a masterly effort and although there was considerable disquiet among certain elements in the Opposition in the way he was proceeding, he was at the heart of the matter and was justified, considering the circumstances, in going about it in the way he did. I hope that, with the improvement in feeling between the Government and Opposition parties, we may look forward to seeing in Trinidad the development of a political system which will be a model of democratic government in that part of the world.

A strong dissenting voice was Norman Pannell, the Liverpool Kirkdale MP, who described the granting of independence to tiny islands as part of a "balkanization of the Caribbean". He, too, foresaw the intractable race problem, noting, "apprehension was strongly expressed by the Indian element". His contribution was dismissed by the next speaker, R. W. Sorensen, the Leyton MP, as "morbid foreboding". For Sorensen, Trinidad and Tobago was "an experiment and a great adventure".

Behind all this, I believe, was an inability to see the colonial as a fellow human being; a wilful exoticisation of Trinidad and Tobago and its peoples; and seemingly the belief that some people were bred for the laboratory, for experiments in multiculturalism, but experiments meant to be kept at a distance. This was the real driver, on the British side, of the independence imperative. Multiculturalism was good for a small, remote and economically vulnerable nation. But for the empire, which had forcibly extracted Africans and seduced Indians from their homelands, had played colonial divide and rule and then left these peoples to sort out their relationships in an economy of scarcity, multiculturalism was not to be countenanced. Instead of giving subjects the right of representation in the British parliament, they were made citizens of small, economically fragile states. Instead of making all subjects full citizens, with freedom to move between the colonies and the ability to name their leader by determining the balance of power at Westminster, they were kept within a ghetto and told they were being gifted freedom.

And despite being told they would automatically receive dual citizenship, many discovered that this was not true. The bill stated that only a person whose father or grandfather was a United Kingdom descendant could qualify. As Vickers noted, illegitimate children were barred from getting dual Trinidad and Tobago/British citizenship under the provisions of the bill. It was an important point: it was very common for children to be born out of wedlock, with no father mentioned on the birth certificate. In one fell swoop, this independence provision disenfranchised many. Hugh Fraser, the under-secretary of state for the colonies, tacitly acknowledged the validity of Vickers' question, but brushed it under the carpet, saying, "On the question of the mother and that of illegitimate children which she raised, I should like to cover those points in correspondence with her."

★

On the morning of Tuesday April 23, 1970, as Trinidad and Tobago's prime minister, Dr Eric Williams, met with advisers to continue efforts to get the Black Power emergency under control, thousands of miles away in London, the UK's prime minister, Harold Wilson, convened his cabinet at 10 Downing Street to consider a special request made by Williams. A UK cabinet minute discloses what was on the agenda. At number three on the table of contents is an item labelled, "Overseas Affairs – Trinidad: Black Power Disturbances". According to the minute, the cabinet was briefed by George Thompson, the chancellor of the Duchy of Lancaster, and Denis Healey, the defence secretary.[44]

Thompson revealed that apparently hours after a dramatic strike action

---

44. Cabinet Minute – CAB 128/45/18 - Record Type: Conclusion Former Reference: CC (70) 18, The National Archives of the UK.

began in Trinidad and Tobago – triggering a state of emergency and eventually coinciding with a mutiny in the Trinidad and Tobago Defence Force – Williams asked Britain for help, "to assist him in restoring order". The details of this request by Williams for foreign assistance were never made known to the public of Trinidad and Tobago.

"The Chancellor of the Duchy of Lancaster said that there have been a series of disturbances in Trinidad instigated by the Black Power movement," the secret Cabinet minute (printed by the UK cabinet secretariat in 1971) recorded:

> The immediate occasion of these had been the trial of Trinidadian students in Canada on charges of arson; but there had been a long-standing background of economic discontent. On April 21, the Prime Minister of Trinidad and Tobago, Dr Eric Williams, had declared a state of emergency and had ordered the detention of 25 Black Power leaders: but ten of these had so far evaded arrest. The situation was complicated by the fact that at much the same time some 50 members of the Trinidad and Tobago Regiment, who sympathized with the Black Power movement, had mutinied and had established themselves in the former United States base at Chaguaramas, where they were holding 200 members of the Regiment as hostages.

Defence secretary Healey also disclosed that Williams had requested help from Venezuela, Guyana and Jamaica. Thompson told those around the cabinet table, "At the outset Dr Williams had asked us to transmit requests to the Head of the Federal Military Government of Nigeria, General Gowon, and to the President of Tanzania, Mr. Nyerere, for the dispatch of troops to assist him in restoring order. He had also sought British assistance in transporting these troops to Trinidad and had asked us to supply light weapons to replace those seized by the mutineers." The UK cabinet minister continued, "Dr Williams had subsequently decided not to pursue his approach to Nigeria and Tanzania; but urgent consideration had been given to our response if he pursued his request for arms."

Thompson made it clear to the cabinet that the UK still had deep economic interests in the island. "Measures were being taken to ensure the safety of the 2,000 United Kingdom subjects in Trinidad. We had major economic interests in the island; and our investment there was estimated at about £150 million [or US $363M." As a context, Trinidad's GDP in 1970 was £340M or US $822M.][45]

Thompson minced no words over the need to keep Williams on the

---

45. Michael Fairbanks, David Rabkin, Marcela Escobari, and Camila Rodriguez, 'Building Competitive Advantages' in Liliana Rojas-Suárez, Carlos Elías (eds) *From Growth to Prosperity: Policy Perspectives for Trinidad and Tobago*, Inter-American Development Bank; 1st edition (June 14, 2006), p. 188 – 190.

UK's side. Though Williams had been forced to turn to the UK for help, the UK politicians still regarded him as a vital leader. The note reads, "Dr Williams was a strong and effective leader, who had considerable influence in the African Commonwealth countries; and it was therefore important that we should do what we could to maintain our relationship with him and to avoid giving him any grounds of complaint."

At the time it was reported that two British warships just so happened to be in the Caribbean Sea. Defence secretary Healey confirmed this was no coincidence: they were sent specifically in response to Williams' request for help. The warships, two frigates, were mandated to remain, "out of sight". The record of the proceedings of April 21, 1970 reads, "The Defence Secretary said that one frigate, *HMS Jupiter*, had been dispatched to Trinidad, with orders to remain 30 miles offshore, and would be in position that night." Further, "A second frigate, *HMS Sirius*, would reach the island within the next two days and would also remain offshore and out of sight. *HMS Jupiter* carried a helicopter and could provide a naval landing party of two platoons trained in riot control. The complement of *HMS Sirius* included a detachment of Royal Marines." In the defence secretary's assessment, the situation created by the mutiny in the Trinidad and Tobago Regiment was serious, since out of a total strength of 700 men 50 were taking an active part in the mutiny and 200 had been neutralised by the mutineers. The mutiny had also left the loyal troops critically short of arms. In Healey's view, "The arms which Dr Williams needed could be dispatched by midnight that night if he so requested: but he now seemed more likely to rely on supplies from the United States. He was also reported to have been promised reinforcements of 1,000 men from Venezuela. Guyana was considering supplying some weapons; but the response from Jamaica, to which Dr Williams had also appealed, was not yet known."

The cabinet minute gives an account of the discussion that then occurred. The key dilemma was balancing the fact that the incidents could potentially upset a region in which the UK still had key economic interests, with the need not to be seen as meddling in the affairs of the newly independent Trinidad and Tobago.

"In discussion, it was suggested that, while the disturbances in Trinidad were on a small scale in terms of the forces involved, the political issues involved could be far-reaching," the document records. "If we were to become involved in the internal security problems of an independent member of the Commonwealth, the consequences might be serious – the more so in that Dr. Williams' Government had already incurred local criticism on the grounds of their alleged reliance on British and American support."

The record discloses that the UK planned, if the situation warranted, to parachute a battalion into the country. The forces which could be provided by their two frigates were too small to be able to exercise any decisive influence on internal security in Trinidad, and if the situation were to deteriorate to a point when it became necessary to intervene to save British lives, a battalion of parachutists could be made available, which could reach Trinidad in two to four days.

The consensus around the table was that it was clearly desirable to avoid such a degree of involvement if possible; British troops should be committed only as a last resort. Some concern was expressed about whether Dr Williams' assessment of the situation was over-optimistic. There was doubt whether he would, in fact, receive from the United States and others the supplies of arms and the assistance on which he appeared to be counting – though indications were that some arms from United States sources could already have reached him.

Harold Wilson, summing up the debate, said the cabinet agreed on the importance of maintaining relations of confidence and sympathy with the Government of Trinidad and Tobago. A serious Black Power revolt would have serious repercussions elsewhere in the Caribbean; and, if these extended to the associated states, it might prove impossible for Britain to avoid intervention. The situation, especially as regards the supply of arms to the Trinidad government, would be closely watched; and, if immediate decisions were required, he himself would need to have discretion, in consultation with the chancellor of the Duchy of Lancaster and the defence secretary, to take necessary action. At the end of the meeting, the UK cabinet –

> Agreed that the Prime Minister, in consultation with the Chancellor of the Duchy of Lancaster and the Defence Secretary, should have discretion to take appropriate action, including the supply of arms, if developments in Trinidad made it necessary to do so at short notice.

All this showed that vital ties remained between Britain and Trinidad and Tobago, notwithstanding independence. Though the new nation has its own anthem, a lovely coat of arms, national birds and a national holiday celebrating its achievement of standing on its own two feet, though it had oil resources and various other forms of wealth, Britain still had a deep stake in the Trinidad economy. The free colony was still producing wealth for its master and its destiny remained inherently bound to British interests. The appearance of freedom masked the fact that while the relationship had ended, the couple remained friends with benefits – but for which partner?

★

The concept of independence is of as little use today as it was in the 1960s. The idea of the sovereignty of small nation states is a pure fiction in a world where the economic prosperity of one country mostly depends on the prosperity of others; where small island development depends to a large extent on direct foreign investment; where multinational corporations often repatriate the bulk of a nation's revenue streams; where oil-based economies are subject to abrupt fluctuations caused by international conflict wholly outside its influence; where indigenous firms are unable to compete with large foreign corporations for lucrative government contracts; where natural disasters and climate change – due to emissions from larger countries – constantly impede efforts at development; where improvements in technology, such as air travel and telecommunications have integrated the social fabrics of nations but done nothing to counter the inequalities between them – in fact accentuated them; and where deep multicultural ties mean states such as Trinidad and Tobago are, in fact, bound up genetically and historically with countries that purport to be estranged from them. Viewed from this perspective, the independence movement of the 1960s appears perverse. It was like asking a cub not to be part of its litter.

Today, it is clear that what British MPs in 1962 regarded as "an experiment and a great adventure" has had dramatically mixed results. Up to 2006, the economy of Trinidad and Tobago remained more or less structured along the same lines as it was in 1962. As some economists remarked:

> Oil income… has not lead to the development of world-class companies. While foreign investment has been consistently high, sophisticated upstream energy industries… have developed little… While depletion of oil or gas is not an imminent threat, it is understood that even the largest reserves will eventually dry up. In fact, the interim sense of economic security derived from this oil and gas windfall has created complacency at the expense of physical and social capital depletion; in fact, Trinidad and Tobago has been decapitalising the country by converting natural resources to currency. Still more troublesome, fluctuating energy prices and substitutes make Trinidad and Tobago's much enjoyed stability largely dependent on external conditions.[46]

Excluding external control of the economy, we might suppose that the good citizens of Trinidad and Tobago have held their own more domestic fate in their hands, with free and fair elections for almost six decades. But, have they? The political system has failed to shed its racial moorings. Political leaders and officials are seldom held accountable on the basis of issues. Instead, no matter how terrible conditions may be in a

---

46. Michael Fairbanks, David Rabkin, et al, 'Building Competitive Advantages' in *From Growth to Prosperity: Policy Perspectives for Trinidad and Tobago*, p. 188 – 190.

constituency, the electors of that constituency will back the party of their race. The result is the failure to address issues such as the structure of the economy and the design of its system of governance.

One of the most bizarre aspects of Trinidad and Tobago's independent life has been its constitution. This seeks to emulate life under the colonial master. Under different guises, there is a king, a house of commons, a house of lords, a prime minister, a civil service. There is a chief justice and a judiciary (lawyers still wear long robes and for a period still donned wigs), yet the country's highest court is still the Privy Council in London. Far from there being effective checks and balances, the prime minister really controls everything. In Westminster style, the prime minister is elected by the people in first-past-the-post elections. They vote for an MP, but, in truth, really vote for the prime minister they desire. The prime minister's MPs control the majority of the house of representatives. That house elects a speaker. It also elects a president who is a ceremonial head of state, akin to the modern monarch at Buckingham Palace. The president is the head of the armed forces, yet must act on the advice of the cabinet, which is led by the prime minister. All the "independent" bodies are appointed by this same president who, in theory, has discretion in some areas, but in practice must consult with the prime minister before making appointments. This president also depends on the cabinet for his budget.

In fact, all the "independent" bodies that are designed to be a check on the power of the prime minister depend on the prime minister for funding, including the elections and boundaries commission, the integrity commission, the police complaints authority and the director of public prosecutions. Even the police service depends on the cabinet for its budget. The police commissioner is appointed in a Byzantine process in which the candidate must get the approval of government MPs. In the past, the political allegiance of the police service was revealed by the fact that the bulk of police officers were "special voters" and on election night the results of the votes among special voters were the first to be publicised. Depending on the margin of the result, all could surmise whom the country's police officers had voted for. Under Dr Eric Williams, this led to a perception of the police service as being supportive of his regime, the PNM, and of one ethnic group – a perception which up to this day is constantly but unconvincingly denied by public officials.

The prime minister not only controls the country's treasury and its legislative organ, this individual heads the security apparatus, following the establishment of a national security council in 1970. The members of that council are all, more or less, appointed by the prime minister. This council includes the country's intelligence apparatus, which means that the entire system of law and order is overseen by a political actor with incredible reach. There is, for instance, limited judicial oversight over the interception of communications. On the surface, the Trinidad and Tobago constitution seeks to persuade that it is an homage to the UK's unwritten constitution – with all its alleged checks and balances. But it is really a cloak for the power of one leader. During the independence era it was easy to overlook such details amid the rhetoric about freedom and the beating of tassa drums.

★

On October 12, 2014, Arthur Snell, the British high commissioner to Trinidad and Tobago, attended a candlelight vigil taking place at a park just adjacent to the high commission's offices in St. Clair. Casually dressed in khaki trousers and a grey polo T-shirt, the diplomat joined hundreds who had gathered to protest the Trinidad and Tobago government's decision to proceed with a highway construction project. That project was opposed by an environmentalist who for the previous month had engaged in a hunger strike. Snell walked among the protesters, taking footage with his camera. It was the last night of his tenure as high commissioner.

Yet, if he left Trinidad and Tobago in body, Snell does not seem to have left in spirit. Three years later, he was once more at the centre of discourse on Trinidad and Tobago affairs. This time, in a Facebook comment, he responded to the brutal murder of an elderly curator and preservationist. His take on the country's crime situation was this:

> Society has to recognise its responsibilities at all levels: in a country where the wealthy pay very little tax and can ensure their children have a cossetted future whilst the poor face constant humiliation and belittling, where Sea Lots can exist only hundreds of metres away from the Hyatt Hotel, anger and cynicism flourish like a malignant cancer. We have these inequality problems too in Britain, no doubt, but not at such damaging extremes.

In Snell's assessment, which was carried in the local media, crime was due to simple factors. "The causes aren't complex," Snell said. "They are banal, but tackling them requires sacrifices that Trinidad & Tobago's society does not appear to be prepared to make."[47] In a swift response, Gary Griffith, a former minister of national security, who would later become the police commissioner, hit back saying, "I beg to differ. There was a strong working relationship with the then administration and the British High Commission."[48] So that even in matters as vital as national security,

---

47. *Trinidad and Tobago Guardian*, September 5, 2017, p. A5
48. See https://www.tv6tnt.com/news/7pmnews/griffith-refutes-crime-passiveness-claims-by-arthur-snell/article_28cc21fc-9429-11e7-81b5-affef8b1973d.html

ties remain deep. Diplomats and government ministers can publicly wrangle over the extent of their cooperation.

I believe we now know enough to say, without a doubt, that the granting of independence was the morally inferior of two options held by the colonialist and an abdication of responsibility – which was not one of civilising natives on the basis of some spurious idea of moral superiority, but rather the responsibility to ensure that complex societies riddled with crippling problems engendered by the colonial era – societies that had been exploited for the generation of wealth, societies in which women and men were subjected to slavery and indenture and all manner of divisive depriva-tion – were able to stand on their own two feet. The reality was that having broken his one-time subject's legs, the master told him to run to freedom.

Having enjoyed considerable gain from economic union with Europe, Britain now finds itself poised, with Brexit, to turn its back on the makings of its post 1970s modern prosperity. As it did with the colonies that helped to build its wealth, Britain now argues for freedom and independence, but in a manner that is as disingenuous as the 1960's independence movement and as obsolete as a solution to contemporary problems. But if it is really the will of the British people to leave Europe, perhaps attention can now be turned to the former colonies gathered together in that union known as the Commonwealth. Now, more than ever, Britain will need to rely on its global ties. Here is a golden opportunity, at last, to forge the deeper integration that should have taken place in the 1960s. Here is a moment to see, at last, former subjects as fellow human beings. Unfortunately, the omens are not good. The cruel disasters of the Windrush scandal – when elderly Caribbean-heritage people were denied their livelihoods and in some cases were expelled from the UK to Caribbean countries they didn't know – indicates too clearly that racial contempt remains at the heart of British Conservative government policy.

II. The Laws of the Free Colony

Sex is everything. Yet in the free colony, it remains policed to the hilt, in law if not in deed. Which is almost worse. Every year there is a carnival, but it is a deceptive masque that at once frees and imprisons revellers given the realities beneath the glitter. One reality is the Sexual Offences Act, Section 13 and section 16:

13. (1) A person who commits the offence of buggery is liable on conviction to imprisonment for twenty-five years.

(2) In this section "buggery" means sexual intercourse per anum by a

male person with a male person or by a male person with a female person.

16. (1) A person who commits an act of serious indecency on or towards another is liable on conviction to imprisonment for five years.

(2) Subsection (1) does not apply to an act of serious indecency committed in private between –
(a) a husband and his wife;
(b) a male person and a female person each of whom is sixteen years of age or more, both of whom consent to the commission of the act; or
(c) persons to whom section 20(1) and (2) and (3) of the Children Act apply.

(3) An act of "serious indecency" is an act, other than sexual intercourse (whether natural or unnatural), by a person involving the use of the genital organ for the purpose of arousing or gratifying sexual desire.

Here we see anal sex is made criminal for both gay and straight couples, though the law is probably of greater significance to gay couples. And the offence of "serious indecency" is broad enough to swallow most other forms of sexual activity, so long as it is not done by heterosexuals. In other words, sex between gays is what is being targeted.

These sections of the act are rarely enforced by the police in Trinidad and Tobago and have been subject to legal challenge. But that is of little comfort. The law is a public declaration of society's values. It is a scarlet letter against the bodies of gay individuals. And contrary to what is often said, law enforcement officers do sometimes enforce the law. Individuals have been charged and convicted of these offences when coupled with other serious crimes. That gays have not been targeted in practice does not reduce the damage done. There is a pervasive, lingering threat of enforcement, looming like the sword of Damocles over the head of the gay citizen. That sense of peril is worsened by repeated failures to repeal the law, giving the impression that the state regards these laws as useful and relevant.

Gay rights are by no means a settled issue in Britain. But in 1967 – five years after the Trinidad and Tobago Independence Act was passed – Westminster decriminalised homosexual acts in private between two men twenty-one years and older in England and Wales. In 1980, Scotland decriminalised homosexual acts, and Northern Ireland followed in 1982.

While Britain has been reforming its laws for the better, independent Trinidad and Tobago was taking steps to entrench homophobia. The 1986 act was amended by different government administrations thereafter – in 1994, in 2000 and in 2012 – without the offensive provisions being removed. In fact, the Children's Act of 2012 further entrenched homophobia in the law by granting children permission to have consensual sex with one another, except male gay children.[49]

---

49. See Children's Act section 20 (1) (c), (2) (c) and (3)(c).

If there was any doubt about the free state's stance on this matter, those doubts were erased by the Equal Opportunity Act of 2000. The act was designed to protect persons from discrimination. But the parliament opted to insert a provision explicitly stating that "sex does not include sexual preference or sexual orientation".[50] Six senators pointed out the injustice. But Ramesh Lawrence Maharaj, the attorney general at the time, said:

> The Government has decided that in the light of the ground-breaking nature of the Bill we should not include this at this time because it should be subjected to further study. In any event, inasmuch as homosexuality has not been decriminalised in Trinidad and Tobago, it cannot be recommended that the legislation extends to protect homosexuals at this time.[51]

Thus, the Trinidad and Tobago parliament passed an anti-discrimination law that discriminated against gays without even having any explicit policy basis for doing so.

It is argued that the Trinidad and Tobago parliament's continued stance against gay rights is an exercise of its sovereignty, and that the country's parliament is accountable to an electorate. Yet, assuming the question of minority rights is a matter for the rule of the majority, there is no evidence that there has been any attempt by parliament to gauge the public appetite on this issue. Most importantly, there is no indication that the state has considered the seriously discriminatory effects of the exclusion of sexual orientation on members of the gay community. That community would, ironically, be better placed had the country remained under British rule. At the same time, the seeds relating to the social norms surrounding homosexuality in Trinidad and Tobago were planted under British colonial rule. Long before the 1986 Sexual Offences Act, the 1925 Offences Against the Person Act contained this provision:

> Any person who commits any act or acts which if done or committed in England would amount to or constitute the offence of murder, manslaughter, buggery or rape, shall be deemed guilty of murder, manslaughter, buggery or rape, as the case may be; and every offence mentioned in this Act which would be an indictable offence according to the law of England shall be and is deemed to be an indictable offence in Trinidad and Tobago.[52]

When Trinidad and Tobago became independent, there was no review of its colonial laws. They remained in force on the assumption that should something need to be changed, the independent nation would be able to

50. Equal Opportunity Act, section 3.
51. *Hansard*, Trinidad and Tobago Senate, Thursday, September 28, 2000, p 752.
52. Section 3, Offences Against the Person Act 1925.

change it. But instead of moving with the world to take steps to eliminate homophobia, the free colony deepened it.

In 1986, the Trinidad and Tobago parliament passed a law banning homosexuals from other countries from visiting. The Immigration Act declared the following prohibited classes: "prostitutes, homosexuals or persons living on the earnings of prostitutes or homosexuals, or persons reasonably suspected as coming to Trinidad and Tobago for these or any other immoral purposes". In 2016, the Caribbean Court of Justice – a regional court set up to adjudicate on a trade treaty – held that this legislation was lawful. In a 28-page ruling, the court expressed no abhorrence to the law and argued it was never implemented because of an apparent, unwritten policy of non-implementation.

Yet, similar provisions of this Immigration Act were implemented in 2010, by none other than Martin Joseph, the country's minister of national security. With a general election looming, Joseph, a member of the ruling PNM, banned the entry of a political strategist working for the opposition UNC. He exercised his power under section 8 (1) (q) to do so.[53] That section empowers the minister to issue an order barring, "any person who from information or advice which in the opinion of the Minister is reliable information or advice is likely to be an undesirable inhabitant of, or visitor to Trinidad and Tobago."

But the laws relating to homosexuality are not the only things that failed to change in the decades since independence. While children are not allowed to engage in consensual homosexual acts, for years they were allowed to marry adults.

Under the Marriage Act, the Muslim Marriage and Divorce Act, the Hindu Marriage Act, and the Orisa Marriage Act, girls as young as 12 years old and boys as young as 16 years old could be married. The laws originated under colonial times when it was the view of the state that religious practices should be sanctioned to avoid hardship. For example, the state often seized the inheritable property of Hindu families whose otherwise inheriting children were deemed illegitimate under the law. When the Hindu Marriage Bill was being debated in Trinidad and Tobago's colonial legislative council, T. M. Kelshall, a council member, said on the first day of debate, "I congratulate the Government on bringing this measure. It is indeed a great step forward." However, the council sensed it was taking one step forward, but two steps back in the matter of the permitted age of marriage. H. Wilcox Wilson, the attorney general, felt the need to justify the 12-year age limit. The best he could do was point out that Muslims had been allowed the same since 1936. E. V. Wharton said, "I think that

53. http://www.guardian.co.tt/news/kamla-gives-minister-week-to-explain-action-6.2.333380.05c622c87b

Government should undertake some educational propaganda amongst these people." Kelshall added, "Perhaps later we shall see what can be done about this question of raising the age."[54] The age limit stayed for half a century. The law was not amended until 2017.

★

Trinidad and Tobago is an independent nation, but you could not tell that by looking at the chapter in its constitution that relates to the judiciary. After sections dealing with the "Supreme Court", "The Court of Appeal", and the "Appointment of Judges" comes section 109; this stipulates that the Judicial Committee of the Privy Council in London is to be the highest court of appeal. It is not for Trinidad and Tobago judges to resolve the most important questions of its jurisprudence; it is not for the chief justice or any other of the members of the "Supreme Court". It is for British overlords.

Section 109 has remained, despite independence. Even when Trinidad and Tobago became a republic in 1976, removing itself from the countries that regard the UK monarch as head of state, this provision of the law was preserved. No other fact better betrays the inherent contradiction in the claims of independence.

The result of this arrangement is an aberration: the democratically-elected leaders of Trinidad and Tobago are subject to the UK's Privy Council. Since all actions by public officials are challengeable in court, if a lawsuit is filed against the Trinidad and Tobago prime minister and the cabinet, the matter is ultimately settled by London. Even when the newly independent nation decided to name its highest award the Trinity Cross, the matter was taken to court decades later and the Privy Council decided the title was discriminatory to members of the local Hindu and Muslim communities since the cross reflected Christian tradition.[55] Even the actions of the ceremonial head of state – who commands the army – are subject to judicial review by the Privy Council.[56] Of course, in most countries the actions of leaders are always subject to review by the courts. The difference here is this review subjects a sovereign jurisdiction to the will of a foreign institution.

The impact of this arrangement is profound, a dramatic example being its effect on the imposition of the death penalty. Successive governments

<hr />

54. *Hansard*, Trinidad and Tobago Legislative Council, Friday 18 May, 1945, pp. 182-189.
55. *Sanatan Dharma Maha Sabha of Trinidad and Tobago Inc & Ors v. The Attorney General of Trinidad and Tobago (Trinidad & Tobago)* [2009] UKPC 17 (28 April 2009).
56. *Attorney-General of Trinidad and Tobago v Phillip* [1995] 1 AC 396 and *Attorney General v Dumas* (Trinidad and Tobago) [2017] UKPC 12 Privy Council Appeal No 0069 of 2015.

have expressed the view that the country's capital punishment law should be implemented. Two successive prime ministers have acknowledged that the death penalty is the law. However, the Privy Council has set down legal conditions that effectively prevent hanging given the lengthy time-line of judicial review processes relating to murder cases. Political leaders have indicated their belief in widespread support for the death penalty, but they have been unable to implement such a policy because of the London court. This, perhaps, is a lucky fact if you regard hanging, as I do, as unacceptable in any humane society, and if you believe, as I do, that matters of human rights should not be resolved by mob rule.

Why has Trinidad and Tobago not removed itself from the Privy Council? What could account for such a ceding of sovereignty? The country's racial politics holds the key.

★

On April 25 2012, a few months before Trinidad and Tobago celebrated its 50th anniversary of independence, Kamla Persad-Bissessar, the prime minister, addressed parliament. She had a birthday gift for the nation.

"The time has surely come for us to review our relationship with the Privy Council," she said. "I am pleased to announce that the Government will be bringing legislation to this honourable house to secure the abolition of appeals to the Privy Council in all criminal matters so that this jurisdiction would then be ceded to the Caribbean Court of Justice [CCJ]."[57] However, she said that though the state would abolish the criminal jurisdiction it would not yet abolish the civil jurisdiction. In her view, though the boat should be rocked, it should not be rocked too much: the Privy Council was still needed for matters of commercial law. Within weeks, however, this confused proposal was dead in the water. It emerged that it was legally impossible for Trinidad and Tobago to partly accede to the Caribbean court without a revision of the regional treaty establishing it.[58]

Over the years, the prime minister's party, the predominantly East Indian-based UNC, has flip-flopped on the issue of the CCJ. The party lobbied successfully to get the court headquartered in Trinidad and Tobago. Yet, it declined to make the court its highest court of appeal. This hesitancy coincided with a period in the 2000s during which the party was thrown into disarray by criminal proceedings being brought against several of its high-ranking members.

57. *Hansard*, Trinidad and Tobago House of Representatives, Wednesday, April 25, 2012, pp. 200-205.
58. See: https://guardian.co.tt/news/2012-07-11/rowley-brands-pm-irresponsible-over-ccj

The party accused the predominantly African-based, ruling PNM of using the courts to prosecute its members. Basdeo Panday, the UNC leader, was among those charged with criminal offences. His conviction for a failure to declare London assets was quashed due to public disclosure of manoeuvres behind the scenes involving the magistrate who presided over his trial, a PNM attorney general and chief justice Satnarine Sharma. It was also later reported that the PNM attorney general had placed some degree of pressure on the office of the director of public prosecutions to act in relation to Panday. Though all parties involved denied wrongdoing, one effect of these develop-ments was to raise question marks about the Trinidad and Tobago justice system and its ability to insulate itself from politics. The Privy Council, in this context, was perceived by the UNC as being something of a neutral zone of safety to which final appeals could be made.

The failure to abolish the Privy Council is thus a direct end-product of two things: a contentious two-party political system aligned on racial lines, and the perception that in Trinidad and Tobago the legal system is vulnerable to political interference.

In terms of the latter, the constitution of the country has entrenched contradictions which make such interference an ever-present possibility in theory, if not in fact. Whilst the office of the director of public prosecutions is envisioned as an independent post, appointed by a judicial and legal service commission, the fact is that the prime minister has a veto over the appointee – and this power has been exercised. This means that whoever fills this supposedly apolitical post must meet the satisfaction of the prime minister of the day. The prime minister also controls the total financial allocation given to the office of the DPP in the annual budget. The special anti-corruption investigations bureau also falls under the office of the attorney general, a post determined by the prime minister.

The entire arrangement is a tinderbox. With politics divided by race, each side mistrusts the other. Since the judiciary's impartiality is also brought into the question, it leads politicians to cling to the UK court which, because it is administered by foreign officials, is perceived to be more likely to be impartial. The absurdity of the retention of the Privy Council must be understood in the context of factors established during the colonial era and then perpetuated by legal provisions formulated during the grand independ-ence era of the 1960s, with the complicity of the British parliament.

By 2009, the problem had come back to haunt the ex-colonial master. Lord Nicholas Phillips, Britain's top judge, was driven to publicly lament the "disproportionate" amount of time the law lords on the Privy Council spend on cases from the former colonies, mostly the Caribbean.[59] "In an

59. http://www.bbc.co.uk/caribbean/news/story/2009/09/090922_privyccjphillips.shtml

ideal world", he stated, Commonwealth countries would stop using the Privy Council and set up their own final courts instead. But life in the free colony is far from ideal.

★

At approximately 8.00 pm on July 27, 1990, while shooting was heard inside and outside of the Trinidad and Tobago parliament, a terrorist ordered the prime minister at gunpoint to instruct the soldiers outside to withdraw and lay down their arms. A.N.R. Robinson, the prime minister, replied, "Attack with full force!" The terrorist shot him in the leg. According to the report of a commission of inquiry held decades later:

> 2.195. Many MPs were beaten and/or injured. Leo des Vignes died from a gunshot wound to one of his legs. Prime Minister Robinson was struck in his head and face, badly beaten and subsequently shot in his leg. Mr. Richardson was struck in his face with the butt of a gun... Mr. Winston Dookeran, the Minister responsible for Planning, was cuffed in his face by an insurgent who callously and facetiously said: "You didn't plan for that though!" Mr. Selby Wilson, the Minister of Finance and the Economy, was beaten about his head and threatened by an insurgent with a gun that he would be thrown through a window. Mr. Trevor Sudama suffered an abrasion from a bullet which grazed one of his feet.

> 2.196. All of the hostages at the Red House were obliged to resort to the most primitive toilet arrangements between Friday and Sunday. Some of the male MPs urinated and defecated on themselves; others used glasses in which to urinate. The Deputy Speaker, Dr. St. George, was beaten and subjected to humiliating indignities...[60]

The July 1990 terrorist attack represented the greatest threat to law and order the free colony has ever seen. Yet the perpetrators of the attack, the Jamaat-Al-Muslimeen, have never been held accountable in court. This is because of the failure of the Trinidad and Tobago judicial system to adjudicate in a timely manner on the question of the legality of an amnesty document and a determination by the Privy Council that given the fact that four years had passed since the events, it would be an abuse of process. Among the offences committed by the group during their attack – which also saw them seize a television station – were offences under the Treason Act, the Firearms Act, the Explosives Act, the Offences Against the Person Act, the Accessories and Abettors Act, the Malicious Damage Act, the

---

60. Sir David Simmons QC, *Report of the Commission of Inquiry of the Attempted Coup of 1990*, available here: http://www.ttparliament.org/documents/ rptcoe1990.pdf

Sedition Act, the Riot Act, the Summary Offences Act, the Larceny Act, and the Military Training (Prohibition) Act.

What has been the effect of this on law and order generally? For some, the fact that a band of men could commit such serious crimes and still walk free set the tone, post-1990, and precipitated the rise of crime in the twin-island republic. But the events of 1990 also laid bare deficiencies in the law itself. In particular, the circumstances underlined the fact that in Trinidad and Tobago no one seems to know what the powers of the country's president really are.

When Prime Minister Robinson cried out, "Attack with full force!" some were of the view that he had no authority to do so. That is because under the constitution it is the president – not the prime minister – who holds, "the supreme command of the armed forces".[61] Yet, the same constitution also stipulates that the president must act on the advice of the cabinet. So while the president has discretion in some specific areas, he or she is in essence a kind of mouthpiece for the prime minister – via the cabinet. In a way, therefore, it was appropriate for Robinson to issue his command, for it was really up to the cabinet to advise the acting president to do so.

But things are more confusing when it comes to the so-called amnesty document that the terrorists obtained from the acting president. This document, essentially a kind of presidential pardon, was clearly procured under duress. The prime minister and dozens of MPs were being held hostage. It was felt by those who oversaw the armed forces during this time that attacking with full force would endanger lives. The signing of the guarantee appeared to be a way to secure the lives of the hostages.

When the state eventually sought to begin criminal proceedings, the terrorists cited this document as a binding legal guarantee that they would not be prosecuted. A presidential amnesty had been granted, they argued. But no amnesty can be granted by an unelected president without the instruction to do so by the prime minister or a minister designated by him. Both the prime minister and the minister of national security were being held hostage at parliament when the amnesty document was signed. In 2012, during the inquiry into the 1990 events, the country's former top judge, Michael de la Bastide, stated it was clear that the constitution did not envision a president simply acting on his own accord.

"When the president is given power, he must act in accordance with the advice of the political directorate," de la Bastide said.[62] "You have to be an ex-colonial to understand the translation." De la Bastide said that focus was

61. See "Cabinet under the gun" Newsday 22, 2012, : http://archives.newsday.co.tt/
/2012/11/22/cabinet-under-the-gun
62. Ibid.

placed on the president, and not the cabinet, who had to give the president the advice to grant the amnesty, adding that "a significant number of cabinet members were under the wrong end of a gun."

A difference in interpretation of the complex law relating to the president's powers resulted in the most egregious assault on democracy ever committed in the free colony going unprosecuted.

Why was a president included in the constitution in the first place? Its drafters arguably sought to have a figure who would function like a monarch. Under colonial rule, people were used to the idea of kings and queens. The presidential address that occurs at the opening of a ceremonial sitting of the Trinidad and Tobago parliament is almost akin to a queen's speech. However, whereas the modern-day monarch reads a speech prepared by the British government outlining its legislative plans, the Trinidad president writes his own speech and can simply mouth off on whatever topic he likes. So in August 2013, President Anthony Carmona called on both political parties to cooperate on crime, made a plea for a referendum to determine the fate of the CCJ, and decried the need for campaign finance reform. The president, who under the constitution is the ceremonial head of the parliament, even reprimanded MPs for their relaxed hours of work, saying, "As the head of Parliament, I strongly suggest that Parliament begin at 8.00 a.m., as we all do in this country, to deal more efficiently and effectively with the nation's business."[63]

This blurring of ceremonial and executive roles has had a profound impact on the everyday realities of political life. One president has delayed the appointment of government senators claiming to have a discretion to do so, another has requested a report from a prime minister on a matter of national interest under a provision of the constitution and another president, Carmona, has even delayed the assent to legislation passed by parliament – representing a stunning frustration of the will of the elected representatives. While some would argue that the president should be a check on the power of the government of the day, the constitution does not state that this is the role of the post-holder.

The hazy areas surrounding the president's powers came to a climax, however, in December 2001 when there was a tie in the election result. The PNM and the UNC each received 18 seats in the house of representatives. It fell to the president, under the constitution to appoint the person best able to command the majority of MPs. The then President, A.N.R. Robinson – the same Robinson who had served as prime minister and shouted "Attack with full force!" during the 1990 terrorist attack – decided he would make a choice. Though the UNC won 50 per cent of the vote, and the PNM 47 per cent, and though the president was urged to maintain

63. *Hansard*, House of Representatives, August 2, 2013, p. 8.

the status quo by returning the ruling UNC prime minister to government, Robinson appointed the PNM candidate. He cited, "moral and spiritual reasons". Those highly personal reasons appeared to trump the will of voters. He had become not only kingmaker, but king.

III. The Price of Independence

On a chilly November day in 2011, Trinidad and Tobago's prime minister was in London. On the agenda was an important meeting at the high commission at 42 Belgrave Square. Kamla Persad-Bissessar, the prime minister, would be meeting with Bob Dudley, group chief executive of BP, formerly British Petroleum, the world's sixth-largest oil and gas company and Trinidad and Tobago's single largest source of government revenue.

The meeting, according to the office of the prime minister, was to discuss, "energy matters related to Trinidad and Tobago and other small Caribbean states." A press release issued after the meeting was more specific. Corporate taxes for 2001 to 2006 had been left unattended by the company. After almost a decade, BP had finally come to a "settlement". The company would pay TT$1 billion, representing "the commencement of payments arising out of the negotiations with the Board of Inland Revenue". BP has been in Trinidad and Tobago for as long as it has been an independent nation. It was set up in 1961 through Amoco Trinidad Oil Company and BP Amoco, producing its first barrel of crude oil in 1972. It is now the country's largest hydrocarbon producer, accounting for more than half of Trinidad and Tobago's national production of oil and gas. It operates 13 offshore platforms and holds an interest in Atlantic LNG, one of the world's largest LNG operations.

Yet, even as it played a crucial role within the local economy, its taxation issues were largely unknown to the general public. At the same time, in its 2011 annual report, BP noted it was a part of an initiative to bolster transparency in the energy sector. "As a member of the Extractive Industries Transparency Initiative (EITI), we work with governments, non-governmental organizations and international agencies to improve transparency in this area. In several countries that are in the process of becoming EITI compliant, BP is supporting the process [...] For example, BP is an active member of the Trinidad & Tobago EITI steering committee."

The 2011 announcement of a tax settlement came months after the fatal Deepwater Horizon oil spill in the Gulf of Mexico had rocked BP. The company was in troubled waters, reeling from the disastrous damage to its image, billion-dollar compensation claims and intense scrutiny over the safety of its worldwide operations. But the Trinidad and Tobago government had confidence in carrying on its relationship with BP.

On 25 July 2011, BP announced that it had been awarded two deepwater exploration and production blocks by the government. The award was for a 100% interest in blocks 23(a) and TTDAA 14 offshore Trinidad's east coast. These blocks increased BP's acreage in the region by 889,000 acres.

For some, BP is part of a never-ending cycle. Small nations are told they need to open their doors to foreign investment. Foreign companies from the former colonial motherlands take root and operate, raising important revenue streams for local government. But after decades, local capacity remains underdeveloped. Independent nations still rely on foreign investment for vital capital.

In 2011, a senior BP official saw things differently. "There are quite a few things that I have observed even in the press about multinationals not working for the country of Trinidad and Tobago, taking things out but not putting things in," the official said. "Without attribution to any specific person, those are the comments that I'm sure others would have seen, and we don't find those particularly helpful or in the spirit of partnership and co-operation."

Such a spirit of partnership and cooperation abounds in companies like Atlantic LNG, in which BP has had a major stake. Atlantic is one of the world's largest producers of liquefied natural gas (LNG). It produces LNG delivered from fields in and around Trinidad and Tobago to a four-train liquefaction facility, located in Point Fortin, on the southwest coast of Trinidad. At one point, the stakes in Train 1 were: BP Trinidad LNG B.V. (34 per cent), British Gas Trinidad LNG (26 per cent), Repsol LNG Port of Spain B.V. (20 per cent), NGC Trinidad and Tobago (10 per cent), Suez LNG Finance S.A. (10 per cent). The stakes in Trains 2 and 3 were: BP Trinidad LNG B.V. (42.5 per cent), British Gas Global Investments B.V. (32.5 per cent), Repsol Overzee Financien B.V. (25 per cent). And the stakes in Train 4 were: BP (Barbados) Holding SRL (37.8 per cent), British Gas Trinidad LNG Limited (28.9 per cent), NGC LNG (Train 4) Limited (11.1 per cent), Repsol Overzee Financien B.V. (22.2 per cent).

While Trinidad and Tobago has a stake in the project (NGC is the national state-owned company), companies from the two countries that once ruled it – Spain and Britain – dominate the list. Much revenue leaves. But small countries have little choice but to depend on big brothers. With independence, a new age of dependency.

A few years after her London meeting with BP, Kamla Persad-Bissessar made an address to the nation when the oil price on which the national budget was based fell from about US$100 per barrel to about US$60 per barrel.

"We shall navigate safely through these turbulent times," Persad-Bissessar said, in a television broadcast as she announced a 15% cut in government spending across various ministries. "Trinidad and Tobago has been here before and was able to overcome the challenges faced. The population can feel confident. We can withstand the low oil prices and the right govern-ment is in place. Today the economy is strong and in good shape." Beneath the prime minister's bluster was a stark decline in revenue reflecting the drop in oil prices. Revenue would fall from TT $45.6 billion to TT$41.3 billion. By the time a new government was in place in 2017, that figure would be about TT$30 billion.[64]

Days before the presentation of the national budget in 2017, Dr Keith Rowley, Persad-Bissessar's successor, would tell the population at a special forum, "The revenue situation facing us in 2018 remains a very challenging one and the government will be taking steps necessary to ensure that it will be tightening its revenue collection mechanisms." He said that energy sector revenue – the single largest contributor of overall revenue – had fallen from TT$19.4 billion in 2014 to $TT 2.1 billion. Saying the economic situation was inherited from the previous government, he called on citizens to make suggestions. With budget day looming, Rowley said, "The country, out of necessity should remain open to any and all sugges-tions to boost revenue levels. We are hopeful that today even at this late stage useful suggestions can still be put forward, if not for Monday but surely for the months and years ahead."[65]

Whatever ambitions both leaders had for their time in high office, both had to come back down to earth. Curiously, while every prime minister has extolled the need to diversify the economy, so that all eggs are not kept in one basket, this diversification process has remained slow. Oil and gas have been the true rulers. And whoever rules these commodities by extension rules Trinidad and Tobago.

★

When Queen Elizabeth II visited Trinidad and Tobago in 2009, she stayed at the Carlton Savannah Hotel. The hotel was brand new. It had wonderful views of the Queen's Park Savannah, the large park at the centre of the capital city of Port of Spain, still named after the monarch. The Queen could look upon her park, which is said to be the world's largest roundabout, and prepare her speech.

Elizabeth II was in town to open that year's Commonwealth Heads of Government Meeting. At the opening ceremony held at the National Academy for the Performing Arts – just across the Savannah – she ad-dressed 49 world leaders, including special guests such as Nicolas Sarkozy, UN Secretary-General Ban Ki-moon, and Danish prime minister, Lars Løkke Rasmussen. The building they all sat in had been constructed by a

---

64. See Ministry of Finance, Estimates of Revenue 2017.
65. See http://www.classifieds.guardian.co.tt/news/2017-09-27/public-must-hold-strain

Chinese firm awarded a contract pursuant to a loan agreement between Trinidad and Tobago and China. Though it featured a striking exterior of glass and steel, from the moment the building opened there were complaints about shoddy construction, poor integration with the surrounding community, and a lack of consultation with the artists whose academy was supposed to be housed there. By 2014, health and safety authorities closed the building for weeks due to a lack of fire safety compliance.

But in 2009 all that glittered was gold. The Queen, having presided over the opening ceremony – the pageantry featured dancers on stilts – retired to her suite. The Carlton Savannah had been finished just in time. Four years later, the same hotel was placed into receivership by a state-owned bank. Its sole function had been fulfilled.

The award of the contract to construct the National Academy for the Performing Arts was just one example of a large-scale project being awarded to a foreign firm. The contract for a new prime minister's residence was awarded to a foreign firm, and many of the other billion-dollar projects in the capital. The complex housing the parliament went to a consortium lead by a foreign contractor. A major highway interchange project was awarded to a foreign firm. It has been stated that foreign firms have the capacity to get the job done. After decades of foreign firms building major projects, local capacity still trails behind. So much so that by 2010, a commission of inquiry into the public construction sector warned of a skewed playing field.[66]

Even as the country literally seeks to build itself, it cannot do so without firms from abroad, firms that have often been awarded lucrative contracts amid whispers about sleaze and kickbacks to the political parties that hand out these contracts. It cannot be denied that the lack of stringent anti-corruption measures in the award of state contracts benefits the many foreign companies that have been awarded billion-dollar contracts. The fact that after five decades, local construction lags far behind is demonstration enough that the benefits local workers might enjoy by being employed by foreign firms remain shallow and transient.

Another way of looking at it: the free colony is a feeding ground for international companies looking to cash in. Independence handed the colony right back to those who, like Columbus, claimed divine right over it.

---

66. See the *Report of the Commission of Inquiry into the Construction Sector* http://www.ttparliament.org/reports/20100406-CommEnqConstSect.pdf

THE AGONY AND ECSTASY OF ERIC WILLIAMS

On March 22nd, 1981, Mongolia sent a man into space; John McCain's father died in a military plane; the top song in the US was "Keep On Loving You" by REO Speedwagon; British summer time began, and Eric Williams sat at his desk to make the last entry he would ever make in his diary. In a list of expenses he incurred during the course of that Sunday, Trinidad and Tobago's first prime minister – who had taken the country from colonialism to independence – itemised one final payment. He wrote: "Insurance $320.00".

We know this only because of the invaluable resource that is the Eric Williams Memorial Collection, an important archive of Williams' books, papers and memorabilia housed at the University of the West Indies (UWI) in St. Augustine, Trinidad. Williams was a trailblazing politician known in international circles, but he was also a historian of considerable repute who wrote books that are today regarded as fine examples of both historical and memoir writing. *Capitalism and Slavery* and his autobiography *Inward Hunger* are classics.

His fame notwithstanding, many uncertainties exist about Williams. One thing, though, is not disputed: he was meticulous. He kept diaries spanning decades, detailing what time he woke, when he went to bed, where he dined, his blood pressure, the books he read, the books he wrote, the music he listened to, the groceries he bought, when he got a haircut and even how much money he gave to church collections. Because of these diaries, we know that Williams' famous hearing aid cost him US$400 in 1976; his spectacles $187.

But in the final week of his life, for reasons best known to himself, Williams declined to make any further entries in the blue, gold-lettered British West Indies Airways diary he had been using. After a lifetime of writing everything, he wrote nothing for the seven days leading up to his death on March 29, 1981. This suggests his death was not a result of an abrupt illness that caught him off guard. It suggests that the final entry of "Insurance $320.00" was meant to be momentous.

This detail is an example of the profound insights literary archives supply. It adds considerable weight to the notion Williams was preparing for the end, turning the theory that he committed suicide into an almost irresistible inference. In the days after his death, reports emerged that he had paid off his house staff. It is also said that he discovered he was a diabetic but maintained the habit of making "huge daiquiris" heavily sweetened with syrup, drinking large glasses of coconut water thickly sweetened with glucose, and never leaving untouched the pieces of cake served in Parliament during the tea-break.

Most tellingly, at the height of his distress in March 1981, Williams reportedly refused to see a doctor. If true, this was a striking about-turn for a man who, according to the archive materials, sometimes saw three doctors a day, often mere hours apart. The materials give us a dizzying roll-call: Dr Bartholomew, Dr Aqui, Dr Lee, Dr Mc Shine, Dr Joseph, Dr Wyke, Dr Ince, "some Japanese doctor". The records also indicate how Williams was friendly with physicians all his life, dining and having drinks with them and their spouses. In fact, his closest friend for most of his life was a doctor, according to some accounts lodged at the Memorial Collection.

Therefore, an advanced directive from Williams, the sitting prime minister, to the effect that no doctor was to see him was completely inconsistent with his lifelong reliance on medical professionals. Either something overwhelmingly powerful was operating in his mind in the last week of his life (mental stress? paranoia?) or the accounts of his final days have been seriously tampered with.

If Williams' death was enigmatic, so was his life. For instance, the diary entries suggest that in 1976, the year Trinidad and Tobago became a Republic, Williams paid one of his ministers, John O'Halloran, a total of $1,244 for drugs. The following is recorded:

January 17, drugs, O'Halloran – $100.00
February 10, drugs, O'Halloran – $100.00
February 23, drugs, O'Halloran – $40.00
March 29, drugs, O'Halloran – $145.00
April 28, drugs, O'Halloran – $107.00
June 4, drugs, O'Halloran – $100.00
June 10, drugs, O'Halloran – $25.00
July 12, drugs, O'Halloran – $100.00
July 13, drugs, O'Halloran –$93.00
November 4, drugs, O'Halloran – $214.00
December 1, drugs, O'Halloran – $220.00

The nature of these drugs is not specified, though it is clear the expense was incurred regularly. At that date, there were roughly $2.5 TT to the USD. In 1975, annual US per capita drug expenditure was $37 US. These were clearly not paracetamol or cough linctus. What were these drugs? Was this expenditure for some controlled substance? Who was this O'Halloran? And why did Williams entrust him with the task of procuring these items? Various reports describe Johnny as having a beautiful voice and beautiful large brown eyes. He wore only white or cream-coloured suits, drove large American cars, had Irish charm. Not only did Williams put him in Cabinet, he fought for him. When

O'Halloran was enmeshed in a corruption and bribery scandal that many regard as a blot on Williams' legacy, Williams kept him. Further, he made him executor of his will. Why?

Whatever the nature of the relationship, nothing could cure what they had. On November 11, 1976, after paying Johnny $214.00 for drugs, Williams underwent an electro-cardiogram, according to the diaries. Something was happening to his heart. Or was something happening to his mind? In 1991, doctors in Japan discovered that you can die from a broken heart. Williams had many doctors.

Is it not fitting for historians to now reassess the nature of the relationship between these two men?

And is it not worthwhile to inquire into the possible impact of drugs on Williams? By the 1980s, the notion of drug use among Trinidadian politicians was hardly new. Two decades prior, senior figures had raised questions about pethidine, a pain medication that was for a time wrongly thought to be safer and not addictive in the way that morphine was. Bhadase Maraj, the opposition DLP party leader who was also famous for having a burly wrestler physique, was said to be addicted to the drug in the years before his demise. Could Williams have had a similar addiction? Long-term pethidine use, when combined with other medications to treat depression or anxiety, can trigger bouts of sweating, agitation, and, eventually, coma—all of which happened to be part of the narrative of Williams' final days.

All of this emerged when I was commissioned by the Bocas Lit Fest for an event on the importance of archives. I was given the option of writing fiction, poetry or nonfiction. But first I had to decide what I would write about. And who.

There were many options: I flirted with archive materials held at the National Library, relating to poets like Derek Walcott and Anson Gonzalez. I gave sweet-eye to Sam Selvon at UWI. Sent a few love notes to the National Archives. Sometimes access was easy, sometimes it was hard. I didn't know what I was looking for, felt my way through the materials. Until I came to Williams. Or rather came back to him: I'd done research at the Eric Williams Memorial Collection for previous writing, had worshipped at the altar of *Capitalism and Slavery* for years. I was fascinated by the man, the unsolvable puzzle of his life. The choice became clear.

But it was one thing to read his books, another thing to hold his diaries in my (gloved) hands, pressing into the plush, padded covers of some of them, feeling the weight of the pages, seeing his handwriting, so consistent, getting a sense of the amount of time he spent in isolation making these same diary entries, his reading habits, his private practices and quirks.

I know archives cannot tell us everything. With their emphasis on the curation of the individual, they are a kind of social media before social media, revealing information but also finessing it, fitting it into a preordained structure and narrative.

In the end, I adopted the vehicle of the investigative poem, a mode I experimented with in my book *Pitch Lake*. Poetry, after all, has a way of simultaneously illuminating and concealing; leaving room for the expression of epistemological problems that confront us when we seek to unearth the truth at the core of any life. After a long period of doing nothing but making notes, my poem, "The Agony and Ecstasy of Eric Williams", came in a torrent of writing. One careful note in a diary was the source of something unknowable, volcanic.

MICHEL JEAN CAZABON – A CENTO

What's your vision of a "typical" Cazabon painting? It may well be a stream glinting under arabesques of bamboo, while one or two white-clad figures wend their way through the middle distance, their unspecified labours – scrubbing rich people's dirty linen in the river, perhaps – now happily at an end for the day.

The reason I ended up going with that name is that I set the whole feeling and design of the band in that era late 1800s, early 1900s. It was the most beautiful time – art was fabulous, fashion was glorious, the architecture was amazing and full of such intricate details – so the name for my Carnival band for 2017 is *Cazabon – The Art of Living*.

Nineteenth-century writers remark on how ragged the Indians were and in what squalid conditions they lived, on or off the estates. They were looked down on even by those who had until recently been slaves.

The First Peoples were barely considered human; those who survived genocide, disease or being worked to death lived wretched lives corralled in "missions" or had fled into the bush. Then there were the Africans, who had been brutally uprooted, transplanted and enslaved.

The Cazabons were slave-owners themselves until not long before they sold their estates at Corinth in 1837, three years after the declaration of forthcoming emancipation.

His family were free coloured people ... free coloured people did not have the same rights and freedoms as whites, though of course they were far better off, legally and materially, than black people.

Although Cazabon was commissioned to make portraits, or painted "types" like mulatresses, he was interested in places, not people.

The presence of the human figure in plein-air landscape painting is very common. It can be a device to make the viewer pause, be entertained by an anecdote.

In "East Indian Couple, Northern Range Beyond", he impressively captures the beauty and light of the plains of central Trinidad, of the distant blue hills of the Northern Range, the contrast of richly dark tree shapes against this light and of the changing tones of our sky.

The painting originally known as "Coolie Group" (now politely rechristened "East Indian Group") shows a serene couple and their child.

His lifelong dedication to his art and his extreme productivity prove that he was driven, that he must have had a vision.

In the end, we are left with several questions which the lack of detailed information about his life makes it difficult to answer with certainty.

From her letters, later lodged in the
Bodleian   Library,   Oxford
University, it is known that in 1849
Mann signed up for some three
months of drawing and painting
lessons with Cazabon. The
association of Mann and Cazabon
did not last long – one month of
lessons were enough for Mann to
conclude that he was a narrow-
minded, conceited man.

The question of how many of the
watercolours gathered in the album
are her own work, and how many
are her teacher's must remain, for
the time being, unresolved.

But the nostalgia evoked by
Cazabon is for a Trinidad that may
never have existed. And the more
you look at his paintings the odder
they start to seem.

The artworks functioned as
recordings of events, advertisements
of commercial possibilities, and
marine and scientific studies. Their
production, substantially different
in nature, form and quality from
the art of the Parisian salons, was
instrumental in the visual projection
of imperial power in the region and
in Europe.

Because his work is often so
accomplished, it's easy to be so
beguiled by his paintings that you
hardly notice what

isn't there

who

BRUEGEL

The bitter winters of the Little Ice Age had an impact on Renaissance culture. Because of colder temperatures, the wood used by violin-maker Antonio Stradivari was denser. The tone of his instruments changed. Fashion adapted. Buttons and buttonholes became popular because they made clothing snug. Painters, including Bruegel the Elder, began to paint the icy scenes unfolding around them. Landscape was no longer depicted as a terrain for the gods. It was a subject in and of itself.

The Belgian winter beginning in the year 1564 was particularly momentous for Bruegel. It came soon after his first son was born and just one year after he married his wife in Brussels. By the time the river Scheldt froze over at Antwerp, the painter was evidently overcome with feelings and sensations alien to him. The world was changing. And changing fast. When huge icebergs from the North Sea floated into Delfshaven Harbour near Rotterdam, it was yet another sign that life would never be the same.

The bitter weather matched the mood in the country. The ascension of Philip II of Spain brought upheaval. There was resentment over taxes. A feeling of estrangement compounded this: it took four weeks to get a reply when requests were sent to the throne. And then Philip sought to revive his father's brutal Inquisition. Protestantism was on the rise and the Spanish monarch would have none of it. It was a return to brutal rule by an alien master.

From afar, Bruegel's winter paintings belie the turbulence that gave birth to them. But look closer and complexity rises to the surface. The paintings present landscape in a new way, anticipating a world filled not with gods, but with mortals whose security is constantly under threat; a world where death could happen at any moment as people go about their daily routine. These are paintings that anticipate an age of terror.

A few years after executing his great icescapes, Bruegel was dead. There are no precise records of what he died of. All we have is a date: December 5th 1569. He was buried at the Church of Notre Dame de la Chapelle in Brussels. He was 44, the winter of his life over.

★

Were it not for the title you might miss it. We are enchanted by the gingerbread houses, the roofs covered in snow-frosting, the delicate trees that have shed their leaves, the large surface of the river, the men, women and children playing games on the ice. But look closer and a church splits the canvas – one of Bruegel's smallest – and to the right a strange object seems to defy the laws of physics: it does not fit neatly into the overall perspective. In *Winter Landscape with Skaters and Bird Trap*, dated 1565, the painter gives us a scene that could have come straight out of the harsh winter of 1564. But look closer and you will notice more than one deadly thing. A small hole has opened on the icy surface of the river to the left. Skaters become birds. The birds, souls. We are being shown how easily pleasure can slide into damnation. The beautiful surface of the ice is a deception. There are terrible currents flowing beneath.

That is one way of looking at it.

Another is that pleasure and pain must coexist. Life is a balance between both extremes. There is no lesson or moral being depicted, only cold, hard facts. In between the joyous and the everyday there is suffering. The painter is simply a reporter. Thus understood, it is a trap to think about the painting as a didactic allegory. The church is shrouded in mist and dwarfed by trees to signify the wrongness of preaching against the sensual. What we better get accustomed to, Bruegel says, is the danger in everything we do, a danger that haunts even the most simple of activities. At any moment a trap could spring.

And another way of looking at it: at any moment a trap could spring but what are we to do about this? Do we cower and hide? Do we remain locked inside our homes, iced-over by snow? No. We defiantly come to the river. We flock. This is a paean to resilience. In the context of the political, economic and religious turmoil of the Little Ice Age, Bruegel is providing a manual for survival. He is making a case for the continued pursuit of happiness. This is something we can relate to today.

★

Whereas a sense of menace is evenly matched with a sense of fun in *Winter Landscape with Skaters and Bird Trap*, in *The Hunters in the Snow* an encroaching danger is given pride of place. A pack of hunters dominate the foreground. They are high up, on a hill overlooking a village in the distance. The anonymous men are accompanied by hounds that still seem hot on the trail. In the distance we see a frozen body of water. Small figures are barely discernable. Perhaps the hunters are returning after an unsuccessful expedition (they carry little evidence of a successful outing). But there is another possibility. Who are these hunters hunting? They are given a bird's eye view of the villagers in the distance. With their weapons, they have the advantage of their dominant vantage point. They have a power of surveillance over the dwarfed figures idling leisurely on the ice.

Bruegel is warning that danger can be hidden and can operate seemingly from afar. In this painting he is less concerned with our willingness to appreciate the dark side of life than our ability to comprehend the true nature of the world.

By the time we get to *The Census at Bethlehem*, from 1566, the dangers are no longer allegorical or just beyond sight. Bruegel transposes the Biblical tale of how Caesar Augustus ordered "that all the world should be registered", prompting the journey made by Joseph and Mary to Bethlehem. What matters most here are not the details of the Biblical story, but the fact that leisure has been overtaken by administration. Whereas the skies in the previous paintings were bright, suggesting a beauty that made the winter bearable even amid nebulous threats, in this painting all is drudgery. The sun is dismal blood red as it sets. A sign bearing the Habsburg double-headed eagle is visible on one building, making it clear where Bethlehem really is. By the next winter painting, *Massacre of the Innocents*, the banal administrative drudgery has transformed into an all-out campaign of murder.

This time, Bruegel had turned away from the dark dismal shades, presenting scenes of horror in bright red, white and blue. Perversely, the painting has the palette of the perfect Christmas card. But all over we see evidence of King Herod's brutal edict that all the infant children of Bethlehem below the age of two be executed. All of this resonated with the politics of the time, when Flemish villagers were attacked by Spanish soldiers under a new administration. All Christmas joy has been forced off the canvas in this painting. Gone are the scenes of women, men and children playing on lakes. The ice has broken.

What makes this painting even more chilling is that there are two versions of it. One is in Vienna and shows the scene in all its literal horror as Breugel painted it. The other version, in London, the Hapsburg state had repainted after Breugel's death. Images of slain or about to be slain infants have been covered over by an odd array of objects – in one case a ham, in another a whole cheese – or animals as substitutes for the children. It has been redacted.

★

It was a bright winter day and I was in Brussels again. I had a few hours of free time before meeting an old college friend, and so decided to visit the Royal Museum of Fine Arts of Belgium. I wanted to see one painting in particular, Bruegel's *Landscape with the Fall of Icarus*.

No one tells you about the simmering doubts behind these quiet paintings, the epic arguments over authenticity, the bitter debates over chronology, the feuds over symbolic interpretation. There is some doubt about whether the *Landscape with the Fall of Icarus* hanging in the museum was done by Bruegel. The painting may be a copy of a lost work. There is also a mystery over the source of light in the painting. It does not appear consistent with sunset. There is a shepherd boy looking up at nothing in the sky. The same museum houses a second version where there is no setting sun and Icarus' father is still in the air, drawing the gaze of the shepherd boy. As stable as these iconic images may seem, the finer points about their provenance are still being discovered.

Walking through the museum's marbled halls, the paintings demand consideration as material objects. They are painted onto various surfaces: oil on wood, tempera on linen, distemper on canvas, prints. Layers dry, varnishes are applied. Colours can change – sometimes subtly, sometimes in major ways. The painting never takes a final form, it is forever fungible. It changes as the paint dries and then it changes as the years pass, revealing undertones and brush strokes, dimming bold swathes of colour under the wear and tear of time. Its molecules are restless, its transformations subtle and infinite. The *Mona Lisa* is changing from moment to moment in ways the naked eye is unable to appreciate. Those of us who are lucky enough to see it today most certainly have not seen the same thing that stood before the world in 1517.

The *experience* of seeing a painting is also forever changing. In a single moment, hanging in a room and visible from several vantage points, it is perceived differently. Light bounces off it from different points, persons approach it from different angles. As John Berger observed, one person may see different things over different times. Entire societies and cultures will look at a single piece of art differently, and we have no reason to believe any of these independent perceptions are invalid. They constitute the painting as much as its particles.

We experience a painting in a moment in time, in our memory of the past, and perhaps through several encounters over time. In this way, the painting breaks down the essence of the now in a way that destroys the idea of time. When you look into Bruegel's paintings, you are swallowed by symbols and truths that were just as true in 1564 as they are today. That is why, despite all of the questions lingering over *Landscape with the Fall of Icarus*, poets like W.H. Auden and William Carlos Williams have been moved to compose lines in response. We know enough of the essence and the truth represented by the painting. We recognize the suffering Auden speaks of and what Williams calls "the whole pageantry" of society: its diversions and preoccupations; how the significant can be made insignificant; and how the insignificant is venerated; how all of this confusion is a kind of absurdity, anomie.

In an essay entitled, "The Origin of the Work of Art", the German philosopher Heidegger wrote that the essence of art is poetry. And poetry is a kind of creation and destruction: a give and take that reveals through concealment. I get a sense of poetry from Bruegel's art because of how it seems to refer to a past and a present simultaneously. In his paintings you can interpret everything as ciphers for the political turmoil of the wintry 1560s. But standing as I did in the heart of Brussels in February 2017, a year after the UK's Brexit vote, a year after horrific terrorist attacks on the city, one could not help but see modern dangers lurking everywhere – in the bird traps, ice holes and distant hunters. And who can see *Massacre of the Innocents* without also seeing photographs of children being herded into World War 2 concentration camps? These paintings have travelled through time. They reveal the world's precarious carnival of life and death. Was this what Bruegel thinking when he painted *The Magpie on the Gallows*?

He told his wife to keep this odd painting for herself. We are given a clearing in a woodland just beyond a village. Safely hidden among the trees, villagers play music and dance together. In the distance are signs of industry and power: a port, a castle, a mill. The villagers seem oblivious to an incongruous object in their midst. A gallows, rendered by Bruegel with light and shadow in a surrealist manner that makes it an impossible object; it stands tall, dwarfing a nearby cross. A magpie is perched on the machine of death, as though it is just a tree. There is a morality tale here. The gallows is a warning of the consequences of too much pleasure. It is also a symbol of death more generally. It is a reminder of the short-lived nature of all fun. But something else is on Bruegel's mind. Consider the strange distortion of this central object, its placement at the centre of the panel as though a doorway. Consider the painting's status as one of the last done before Bruegel's death. Was the impossibility of the deathly gallows not meant to mirror the impossibility of paintings themselves? Their grand illusion? The way they stay alive even after death? Their ability to travel, unlike the body, through centuries? Their never-ending winter? In some ways, Bruegel anticipates that other famous Belgian painter, René Magritte. Like Magritte, he is not concerned with the reproduction of particular scenes. Rather, he seeks the general essence of things. This involves a prioritisation of poetry and allegory over all else. Even in ordinary scenes there is a precarious blend of faithful representation with the surreal. And so an impossible object sits at the centre of the dance in *The Magpie on the Gallows*; a phantom leg appears at *The Peasant Wedding*; and a town is a habitat for symbols in *Netherlandish Proverbs*. Elements of a key early work, *Twelve Proverbs*, are replicated throughout Bruegel's oeuvre. The strange arrangement and allegory of two of Bruegel's last paintings, *Land of Cockaigne* (1567) and *The Beggars* (1568), show that he was a key precursor to the Belgian surrealist movement that would find its fullest expression centuries later. This was another way he found to travel through time.

★

About fifty years before Bruegel's winter paintings, Sir Thomas More was in Leuven. More had travelled to the old university town outside Brussels during a stint as envoy for Henry VIII. More was a close friend of the Dutch scholar and humanist, Desiderius Erasmus, who lectured at the University of Leuven. It was in Leuven that More published *Utopia* in 1516. Although written in a half-serious, half satirical vein, its implicit premise of spelling out what an impossibly good society might look like remains influential. In a new era of turmoil and uncertainty in the Low Lands, the sense of a society wrestling with its ideals is still palpable.

Bruegel's paintings give us news about changes happening around him. And they also serve to ask questions about values that were structuring society ever more rigidly. In this vein, it is no coincidence that he painted *The Tower of Babel* at least three times. His first rendering is lost. But we have two versions, painted in the same year, that tell us something about how he perceived the world around him. Each version presents the Biblical story of how mankind united to build a tower to heaven – until God devised the plurality of languages to divide the human race.

In one version, sometimes called *The (Great) Tower of Babel*, the tower is a sad relic of an ambitious dream. It appears unfinished, unstable and unpleasant. A regal figure, believed to be Nimrod, is in the foreground. He is venerated. His political power appears to be manifested by the feat of the tower itself. But this is a kind of sad commentary. For the tower, though showing glimpses of beauty and accomplishment, is a mess.

In the second version, *The (Little) Tower of Babel* there is none of this complication. The tower rises as powerfully as its ambition. Individual human beings are insignificant. Taken together, both versions present a dichotomy between an ideal and reality, much in the manner of More's *Utopia*, the title of which means "no place", but which sounds a lot like *Eutopia* or "good place".

The contrast between these two versions does more than dramatise the dynamics of the Biblical story. They relate to the religious, political and economic upheavals reshaping society around Bruegel during the 1560s. Labour is presented here, as it is in the rest of the painter's output, as a dehumanising force. Society is bending into a new shape, but there are growing challenges to the freedoms enjoyed by the human spirit. Bruegel is questioning what society should venerate; or at the very least he is setting out the price of the changes happening around him. Part of the pathos of *Landscape with the Fall of Icarus* is in how the preoccupation with short-term forms of work blinds all from seeing the figures taking flight. The human spirit is left with nowhere to soar to, nothing to scale. And no one to lament its downfall. And when there is icy pleasure, death is not very far away. Perhaps Bruegel is simply reporting faithfully what he perceives around him. Or maybe he is inviting us to imagine some other space where birds fly free without fear of traps. A place in the far distance, beyond the ports and horizons of his pictures.

CRUSOE'S ISLAND

There's an island near Chile named Robinson Crusoe Island. But the name is misleading. Robinson Crusoe Island is not really Robinson Crusoe's island. That honour belongs to Tobago, the island next to Trinidad. We know Tobago is the real setting for Daniel Defoe's novel because he tells us so. The book's subtitle places the action in "an uninhabited Island on the Coast of America, near the Mouth of the Great River of Oroonoque". This rules out any of the islands off Chile. More corroboration comes in the text itself. At one point Crusoe asks his subject Friday to explain where the island is in relation to the mainland. From what Friday says, Crusoe ascertains a strong current nearby is tied to the island's position and states:

> I afterwards understood it was occasioned by the great draft and reflux of the mighty river Orinoco, in the mouth or gulf of which river, as I found afterwards, our island lay; and that this land, which I perceived to be W. and NW., was the great island Trinidad, on the north point of the mouth of the river. (p. 111)

Look this up on a map and Tobago is the irresistible inference.

It's true that in a sense it doesn't matter: any deserted island will do for the purposes of the story. It's also true that Defoe was a writer and writers transpose things. But even if that's the case, even if there is a real-life story of a Scottish seaman left marooned near Chile that inspired him, the author's setting is clearly, carefully specified. Walking around Tobago three-hundred years after the novel was published, it's easy to see why he went through the trouble.

There are parts of Tobago untouched for centuries. A few decades after *Robinson Crusoe* was published in 1719, the forest that forms the spine of the island was officially declared a protected area in 1776. At the time, the island was a British colony. (It changed hands no less than 33 times as Courlanders, Dutch, English, French, Spanish, and even Swedish forces fought to colonise it.) The Main Ridge is said to be the oldest reserve in the western hemisphere. There are about 160 species of trees, at least 16 can be found nowhere else. When you walk through this ancient forest, the cool air is filled with a woody incense. The forest is on a high volcanic ridge. A mist falls, a miasma, as the primeval trees stand like sentinels, guarding some dark, hidden nirvana. A sap-sweet fragrance lures you to come deeper, yet parts of the mountain terrain are impassable. I see Crusoe here, trying to make his way through the dense opulence, as small, golden frogs look on from the mulch, brooding, indifferent to his fate.

But the idea of Tobago as a perfectly preserved Eden is also something of a myth. When hurricane Flora hit in 1963, about 75 per cent of the forest was destroyed. What survives is an echo of what was left in 1963. And with its international airport, roads, ports, real estate developments, and coastal resorts, the Tobago of the 18th century has been recast in concrete.

This is the lesson of *Robinson Crusoe*. Wherever placed, whether in the imagination or in a physical geography, the story is a fantasy. In James Joyce's diagnosis it is a particularly English fantasy, a colonial delusion, an imperial project, a vision of self-mastery and conquest. Perhaps the book was meant to be a paean to privateering. Perhaps it was conduct literature: designed to excite recruits to serve their country on the high seas.

Unlike Joyce, I see the Crusoe fantasy as something that sails across nationality. It is a virus, a constellation of malarious ideas: the Utopian notion of a pure, untouched land; the image of a man-god in Eden; and the dream of the all-conquering male in virgin terrain. There is something of this Crusoe contagion lurking inside the very idea of nationalism. He represents the idea of being singled out for survival, of being able to master a plot of land bestowed by divine forces. Who is not drawn to this notion of being special? Of possessing, deep down, the power to be one's true master? As Crusoe tells us:

> I was lord of the whole manor; or, if I pleased, I might call myself king or emperor over the whole country which I had possession of: there were no rivals; I had no competitor, none to dispute sovereignty or command with me. (p. 67)

Has Defoe not given us the seed of the American Dream? The prototype for Daniel Boone? (Thomas Jefferson reportedly read *Robinson Crusoe* twice.) Is this not why walls are now necessary to keep intruders out? Does the Crusoe dream not underlie the desire of nations to preserve their purity? To leave larger political groupings? Europe? Is it not a good reason to oversimplify history? To erase competing moral and legal claims to wealth, resources, land?

The veneration of toxic masculinity, too, is there for all to see. In stating he is a symbol of British conquest, Joyce observes how Crusoe is ship-wrecked on a lonely island with nothing but a knife and a pipe in his pocket, yet becomes an architect, carpenter, knife-grinder, astronomer, baker, shipwright, potter, saddler, farmer, tailor, umbrella-maker. All the Anglo-Saxon soul is in Crusoe, virile independence, unthinking cruelty, persistence, slow yet effective intelligence, sexual apathy, practical and well-balanced religiosity, calculating dourness. Animals are skinned, mutinies engineered, people killed.

The fusion between Crusoe as imperialist and Crusoe as male ideal is captured perfectly by Jules Fesquet's 1877 drawing in which Crusoe becomes Hercules. Instead of being a comic figure wearing a hodgepodge of goatskins, he becomes a cocky jock holding an oversized penile sword. This is very well sketched. It matches the book, where all Crusoe's relationships are subordinate to the pursuit of maleness masked as survival. There's so much testosterone we barely notice when he marries. The marriage is brief, his wife is quickly killed off. Little wonder J.M. Coetzee, in his fictional response *Foe*, is moved to invent a female character, one who is marginalised, excluded from the story by its writer, much as Friday, in Coetzee's symbolic retelling, is silenced by having his tongue cut out.

Unlike, say, Prospero there is very little to exonerate Crusoe or make us sympathise with him. He is racist, describes black people as barbarians, brown people as savages. He may have brought about the drowning of a fellow slave to secure his own liberty (he casually remarks "he... swam for the shore, and I make no doubt but he reached it with ease, for he was an excellent swimmer" (13)). He traffics children. He takes money from the corpse of a drowned boy. He takes on slaves and plots to traffic more. He wilfully takes advantage of native populations, trading useless trifles for gold dust.

Outwardly set in his ways, Crusoe's story nonetheless throws up fascinating contingencies. His experiments with moving his camp show how arbitrary his notion of home is. On the island, Crusoe has power that he would not have in England, but he is much more vulnerable in this new space. For all its newfound liberties, for Crusoe at least, the final verdict on the new republic is made by Crusoe's scarcely reluctant departure.

There's similar ambivalence in the book's emotional landscape. Alongside the machismo is a pervasive vein of tenderness. In his film of the novel, Luis Buñuel invents a scene in which Crusoe hangs a dress on a scarecrow then falls under the spell of his own illusion. For a moment, he lights upon the garment with excited desire only to come back to earth with recognition of his isolation. The scene works because we can imagine it happening. Defoe makes plain Crusoe's despair (Sir Walter Scott notes Crusoe becomes "in the highest degree pathetic"). In this context, his feeling for his servant Friday is charged by his desire to connect. Crusoe tells us: "I began really to love the creature; and on his side I believe he loved me more than it was possible for him ever to love anything before" (p. 110). Friday is more than just surrogate for all other people. He comes to represent an ideal bond:

For never a man had a more faithful, loving, sincere servant than Friday was to me: without passions, sullenness, or designs, perfectly obliged and engaged; his very affections were tied to me, like those of a child to a father; and I daresay he would have sacrificed his life to save mine upon any occasion whatsoever. (p. 108)

This contrasts with Crusoe's earlier relationship with another servant, the brave and loyal Xury, whom he sells back into slavery without hesitation: "He offered me also sixty pieces of eight more for my boy Xury, which I was loath to take; not that I was unwilling to let the captain have him" (p. 19). He twice regrets the loss of Xury, but not for emotional reasons but because of the additional labour Xury would have provided, first on his plantation in Brazil, then on the island.

These contradictions, contingencies and ambivalences are symptoms of a structural pattern within Crusoe's character. His frequent veering between extremes connotes a profound fluidity in his personality. He starts off godless, then is converted to the faith. He rebels against his father, then ends up the prodigal son. He despairs of the island, then comes to see it as his kingdom. He is disgusted by the cannibals then changes his mind. He wants to go home then criticises European civilisation. Was he just too mercurial? Or is his propensity for change not a sign of a truly open mind? Here is the glimmer of hope Crusoe gives us.

Karl Marx sees Crusoe somewhat positively, as embodying the potential of commodity production by freely associating men. But we know enough about Marx's ideas to imagine what he would say about figures like Xury and Friday. Both are mere cogs in Crusoe's colonising agenda. Both are treated as commodities, fruits of his labour. In Friday's case, Crusoe's love threatens to disrupt the mercenary nature of the relationship. While that love takes him to Europe, it still does not transform him into a full-fledged man from Crusoe's perspective. Instead of correcting it, love intensifies the failure of Crusoe's imagination, underlines his inability to see human beings around him. Friday remains a servant and a creature right up to the end of the novel when his sparring with a bear literally serves as entertainment for his master. Their relationship mirrors the master-slave trope where masters, abusing power, would fall in love with slaves yet see no inconsistency between their feelings and the racist assumptions of slavery. Friday volunteers to stay with his master, but the terms of their relationship remain fixed in stone.

At one stage Crusoe himself spends two years in bondage, there is little indication that the experience teaches him anything or provokes any sort of crisis of belief the way his island does. Though in so many areas of his life he is able to move between antinomies, he disappoints gravely because of his lack of real change. The glimmer of hope is snuffed out.

This, then, is the telltale heart of the story, which gives us a tantalising glimpse of a faraway land in which Crusoe and Friday stand side by side as equals. But the image soon vanishes like the footprint in the sand.

NOTES

INTRODUCTION

Baudelaire, *Rockets*, translated by Joseph T. Shipley in *Baudelaire: His Prose and Poetry* (New York: Boni and Liveright, 1919), p. 211.

Jürgen Habermas, *The Theory of Communicative Action*, translated by Thomas Mc Carthy (Boston: Beacon Press, 1981).

Marianne Boruch interviewed by Brooke Horvath in *Denver Quarterly*, Fall, 2008, Volume 43, Number 1.

Margaret Atwood, "Kafka: Three Encounters", broadcast on BBC Radio 3 on May 11, 2015.

THE LAST PAGE

W.G. Sebald, *The Rings of Saturn* (London: New Directions Books, 1998).

V.S. Naipaul, *Miguel Street* (London: Picador, 2011 [1959]).

Derek Walcott, *White Egrets* (New York: Farrar, Straus and Giroux, 2010).

Arthur Schopenhauer, *The World As Will And Idea* (London: Kegan Paul, Trench, Trübner & Co., 1909).

Peter Gizzi, *Artificial Heart* (Providence, R.I.: Burning Deck Press, 1998), p. 33.

NAIPAUL'S NIGHTMARE

Patrick French, *The World Is What It Is* (London: Picador, 2008).

Coverage referred to can be found at *The Telegraph,* March 21, 2008, https://www.telegraph.co.uk/news/uknews/1582389/Sir-Vidia-Naipaul-admits-his-cruelty-may-have-killed-wife.html; April 12, 2008, https://www.telegraph.co.uk/culture/books/non_fictionreviews/3672526/V.S.-Naipaul-failing-as-a-human-being.html; *The Daily Mail,* January 30, 2009, https://www.dailymail.co.uk/news/article-1132743/Misogyny-mistresses-sadism-Why-Nobel-prize-winning-author-VS-Naipaul-centre-vicious-literary-war-decade.html; *The Atlantic,* November 2008, https://www.theatlantic.com/magazine/archive/2008/11/cruel-and-unusual/307073/; *The Economist*, April 3, 2008, https://www.economist.com/books-and-arts/2008/04/03/naked-ambition

Naipaul on Jane Austen in *The Guardian,* June 2, 2011, https://www.theguardian.com/books/2011/jun/02/vs-naipaul-jane-austen-women-writers as well as *Letters Between A Father and Son,* London: Picador, 1999, p. 10; on Dickens, BBC News, March 29, 2006, http://news.bbc.co.uk/2/hi/entertainment/4856046.stm and *The Guardian,* September 1, 2001, https://www.theguardian.com/books/2001/sep/01/fiction.reviews1 (where we should note Paul Theroux is writing) but also in *Literary Occasions* (London: Picador, 2004), where he admires early Dickens but expresses dissatisfaction with later Dickens; on E.M. Forster, *A Writer's People* (London: Picador, 2007), pp. 136-137 and *The Guardian,* August 2, 2001, https://www.theguardian.com/uk/2001/aug/02/books.classics; on James Joyce, *Smithsonian Magazine,* December 2001, https://www.smithsonianmag.com/arts-culture/october-surprise-56295081/.

Derek Walcott's essay on *The Enigma of Arrival,* "The Garden Path", can be found in his essay collection *What the Twilight Says* (London: Faber and Faber, 1998), at p. 121.

Salman Rushdie's UK *Guardian* review of the same novel is at *The Guardian,* March 13, 1987, https://www.theguardian.com/books/1987/mar/13/fiction.vsnaipaul.

Diana Athill's essay 'Editing Vidia', was originally published in *Granta* 69, 2000, and republished in May, 2019, in the magazine's 40th anniversary edition.

Chicago Tribune on Naipaul, published on November 9, 2001, https://www.chicagotribune.com/news/ct-xpm-2001-11-09-0111090033-story.html

Adam Low, director, "Arena: The Strange Luck of V.S. Naipaul", BBC Four, 2008.

Jeremy Taylor, "Finding his Centre" in the *Caribbean Review of Books,* November, 2008.

Derek Walcott's 1965 interview with Naipaul can be found in *Conversations With VS Naipaul* (Jackson: University Press of Mississippi, 1997), p. 5.

V.S. Naipaul, *Guerillas* (New York: Vintage International, 1990 [1975]).

Robert Hemenway, "Sex and Politics in V.S. Naipaul", *Studies in the Novel,* Vol. 14, No. 2 (summer 1982), pp. 189-202. Hemenway also quotes Karl Miller. Selwyn Cudjoe pays particular attention to the implications of *Guerillas'* treatment of women and sexuality in *V.S. Naipaul: A Materialist Reading* (Amherst: The University of Massachusetts Press, 1988), in the Chapter "Doom and Despair: The Eternal Condition of Colonial Peoples" at pp. 167-192.

On the difficulties of V.S. Naipaul's relationship with Shiva, see Savi Naipaul-Akal, The Naipauls of Nepaul Street (Leeds: Peepal Tree Press, 2018), pp 112, 130, 164.

V.S. Naipaul, *A Bend in the River* (London: Picador, 2011 [1979]).

V.S. Naipaul, *Half a Life* (New York: Alfred A. Knopf, 2001).

V.S. Naipaul, *A House for Mr Biswas* (London: Penguin Books, 1969).

V.S. Naipaul's "A Flag in the Island", republished in *The Nightwatchman's Occurrence Book* (London: Picador, 2002 [1967]).

V.S. Naipaul, *In a Free State* (London: Penguin Books, 1971).

V.S. Naipaul, *The Middle Passage* (London: Picador, 2001 [1962]).

V.S. Naipaul, *An Area of Darkness* (London: Picador, 2010 [1964]).

ON HENRY JAMES

Henry James, *The Turn of the Screw* (London: Penguin Books, 1994 [1898].

MARK TWAIN'S CORN-PONE OPINIONS

Michel Foucault, *History of Sexuality,* translated by Robert Hurley (New York: Pantheon Books, 1978), p. 93.

DOUBLES

Incidents referred to include those reported at *Global Voices* on October 5, 2012, https://globalvoices.org/2012/10/05/trinidad-tobago-attacked-whilst-eating-fast-food/ and *Newsday,* February 19, 2019, https://newsday.co.tt/2019/02/19/couple-detained-after-doubles-vendors-murder/
.

IN PLATO'S CAVE

Sir David Simmons QC, *Report of the Commission of Enquiry Appointed to Enquire into the Events Surrounding the Attempted Coup d'état of 27th July 1990*, March 2014.

ROMANTICS IN PORT OF SPAIN

Roger Kamien's book is now in its 11th edition, *Music: An Appreciation* (New York: McGraw Hill Education, 2015). Hal Draper's translation of the lines quoted in German: "In May, the magic month of May,/ When all the buds were springing/ Into my heart the burning/ Bright arrow of love came.// In May, the magic month of May/ When all the birds were singing,/ I told her of my yearning/ My longing and heart-wringing."

Soca

The opening sentence owes a debt of gratitude to Ngugi wa Thiong'o who has frequently observed that Trinidad made steelpan music from oil. See *Globalectics: Theory and Politics of Knowing* (New York: Columbia University Press, 2012), p. 4.

Snakes and Ladders

R.P. Hewett, editor, *A Choice of Poets* (London: Nelson Harrap, 1968).

Dylan Thomas: Three Encounters (With Apologies to Margaret Atwood)

William T. Moynihan, "Dylan Thomas' 'Hewn Voice'" in *Texas Studies in Literature and Language,* Vol. 1, No. 3 (Autumn 1959), pp. 313-326, provides an overview of the views on the issue of sound and sense in Thomas's poetry.

John Goodby's *The Poetry of Dylan Thomas* (Liverpool: Liverpool University Press, 2013) notes Robert Graves' views.

Louise Baughan Murdy, *Sound and Sense in Dylan Thomas' Poetry* (The Hague: Mouton & Co., 1966), p. 18.

This essay pays homage to Margaret Atwood's essay, "Kafka: Three Encounters", broadcast on BBC Radio 3 on May 11, 2015.

Ishion Hutchinson

Ishion Hutchinson, *House of Lords and Commons* (London: Faber and Faber, 2016).

Ishion Hutchinson, *Far District* (Leeds: Peepal Tree Press, 2010).

The Poetry Review, Autumn 2017.

The Show Must Go On

Jane King, *Performance Anxiety: New and Selected Poems* (Leeds: Peepal Tree Press, 2013).

Pamela Mordecai, *Subversive Sonnets* (Toronto: TSAR Publications, 2012).

Thom Gunn, "Duncan" in *Boss Cupid* (London: Faber and Faber, 2010), p. 3.

Dylan Thomas, "Poetic Manifesto", *Texas Quarterly*, 4 (Winter 1961), pp. 45-53.

THOM GUNN'S CARNIVAL

Thom Gunn, "The Messenger", *Poetry*, April 1970.

Baudelaire, *Rockets*, translated by Joseph T Shipley in *Baudelaire: His Prose and Poetry* (New York: Boni and Liveright, 1919), p. 211.

Thom Gunn, "The Miracle", from *The Passages of Joy* (London: Faber and Faber, 1982).

Thom Gunn, "The Art of Poetry No. 72", *Paris Review*, Issue 135, Summer 1995.

Mike Kitay is quoted in "A Poet's Life" by Edward Guthmann, *SFGATE*, April 26, 2005.

LANGSTON HUGHES

Langston Hughes, "Tropics After Dark" in *The Collected Works of Langston Hughes* (Columbia: University of Missouri Press, 2001), p. 167.

Arnold Rampersad, *The Life of Langston Hughes, Volume I: 1902-1941, I, Too, Sing America* (Oxford: Oxford University Press, 1986).

Arnold Rampersad, *The Life of Langston Hughes, Volume II: 1914-1967, I Dream a World* (Oxford: Oxford University Press, 1988).

Arnold Rampersad and David Roessel, editors, *Selected Letters of Langston Hughes* (New York: Alfred A. Knopf, 2015).

Rampersad's later comments on attempting to find out if Hughes was gay are quoted in the *LA Times* of June 13, 1991.

Hilton Als, "The Elusive Langston Hughes", *The New Yorker*, February 16, 2015.

IN THE FIRES OF HOPE AND PRAYER

Lauren K. Alleyne, *Difficult Fruit* (Leeds: Peepal Tree, 2014).

Roger Robinson, *The Butterfly Hotel* (Leeds: Peepal Tree, 2013).

HIS FATHER'S DISCIPLE

Martín Espada, *Vivas to Those Who Have Failed* (New York: W.W. Norton & Company Inc., 2016).

Martín Espada, *Zapata's Disciple: Essays* (Cambridge: South End Press, 1998), p. 3.

You Can See Venezuela From Trinidad

For a history of Angostura Bitters see: http://angosturabitters.com/our-story/

Jak Peake, *Between the Bocas* (Liverpool: Liverpool University Press, 2017), quotations from p. 33 and p. 21, see also pp. 92-95.

Paulo Kernahan, "Spit out that pastelle", *Newsday*, March 11, 2019.

The Rightest Place

BBC Four, "Goldsmiths: But Is It Art?", April 10, 25, 2010.

Melanie Archer, "Stranger than paradise", *Caribbean Review of Books*, November 2010.

Carlos Suarez De Jesus, "At the Little Haiti Cultural Center, a world-class exhibit focuses on the art of the Caribbean", *The Miami New Times,* January 14, 2010. https://www.miaminewtimes.com/arts/at-the-little-haiti-cultural-center-a-world-class-exhibit-focuses-on-the-art-of-the-caribbean-6368511.

Benjamin Genocchio, "Colorful, Witty, Noisy: A West Indies Mélange", *The New York Times,* December 4, 2009, https://www.nytimes.com/2009/12/06/nyregion/06artct.html.

An Essay into the Visual Poetry of S.J. Fowler

An example of Fowler's approach is *Aletta Ocean's Alphabet Empire* (Bristol, Hesterglock Press, 2017).

The Secret Life of a Dyslexic Critic

For the review of Marlon James' *Black Leopard, Red Wolf,* see *Newsday,* June 2, 2019.

Boris Johnson in the Eyes of a Poet

UK *Guardian* obituary on Heathcote Williams published on July 2, 2017, https://www.theguardian.com/books/2017/jul/02/heathcote-williams-radical-poet-playwright-actor-dies-aged-75.

Heathcote Williams, *Boris Johnson The Blond Beast of Brexit* (London: *London Review of Books*, 2016). This was reissued in an updated and expanded version as *Brexit Boris: From Mayor to Nightmare* (London: Public Reading Rooms, 2016).

Heathcote Williams, *Whale Nation* (New York: Harmony Books, 1998).

Heathcote Williams, *Sacred Elephant* (New York: Harmony Books, 1998).

Heathcote Williams discusses Abdul Malik in *Royal Babylon* (Warwickshire: Skyscraper Publications, 2016).

Alice Notley, *The Descent of Allette* (London: Penguin Poets, 1992).

THE FREE COLONY

Because of its length, references in this essay appear as footnotes in the body of the text.

THE AGONY AND ECSTASY OF ERIC WILLIAMS

The diaries referred to are housed at the Eric Williams Memorial Collection, Alma Jordan Library, University of the West Indies, St Augustine, Trinidad. Folder 623 contains the diary relating to 1976.

An attempt to uncover John H. O'Halloran's crimes is made in Paul McLaughlin's, "The Final Accounting of Johnny O: How a Toronto CA traced Trinidad's missing millions", *CA Magazine*, 27 November, 1991.

MICHEL JEAN CAZABON – A CENTO

The excerpts beginning "What's your vision...", "His family...", "The First Peoples...", "Nineteenth-century writers...", "The Cazabons...", "The painting...", "Although...", "But the nostalgia..." and "Because his work..." are from "Out of Sight" by Judy Raymond in *Cazabon: New Perspectives* (Port of Spain: Mark Pereira / 101 Art Gallery, 2019).

"The reason I ended up..." is a quotation from designer Brian Mc Farlane at the launch of his 2017 Carnival band. Full *Newsday* report of October 25, 2016: https://archives.newsday.co.tt/2016/10/25/mac-farlane-channels-cazabon/ Mc Farlane later withdrew a section of the band, named "La Belle Dame and Garçon de la Maison" (The Pretty Lady and the House Boy).

"The presence...", "In the end...", "In 'East Indian...'", and "His lifelong..." are from "Reaching for the Light" by Jackie Hinkson, also in *Cazabon: New Perspectives*.

"The artworks..." is from "Looking for Cazabon in His Landscapes" by Kenwyn Crichlow in *Cazabon: New Perspectives*.

"From her letters..." is from "Cazabon's Contemporaries" by Mark Pereira in the same publication.

"The question of how many" is from an introduction by Timothy Wilcox to the Margaret Mann collection, printed in *The Letters of Margaret Mann*, edited by Danielle Delon (Port of Spain: The National Museum and Art Gallery of Trinidad and Tobago, 2008).

Bruegel

Heidegger's "The Origin of the Work of Art" can be found in *Off the Beaten Track*, edited and translated by Julian Young and Kenneth Haynes (Cambridge: Cambridge University Press, 2002), pp. 1-56. Reproductions of all the paintings discussed can be found easily online, by title.

Crusoe's Island

Daniel Defoe, *Robinson Crusoe* (London: Seeley, Service & Co. Limited, 1919 [1719]).

C. B. Daniel and R. Maharaj, 'Tropical Cyclones Affecting Trinidad and Tobago', Port of Spain: Trinidad and Tobago Meteorological Service, 1986. Information on the Main Ridge Protected Reserve in Tobago also taken from http://www.protectedareastt.org.tt/index.php/profile-of-sites/198-main-ridge-profile

James Joyce, 'Realism and Idealism in English Literature: Daniel Defoe & William Blake' in *Occasional, Critical, and Political Writing* (Oxford: Oxford World Classics, 2008 [Lecture, 1912]), pp. 163-182.

Walter Scott's remarks preface the novel in *Robinson Crusoe* (London: T. Nelson and Sons, Paternoster Row, 1876), p. 31.

J.M. Coetzee, *Foe* (London: Martin Secker & Warburg Limited, 1986).

Karl Marx, *Das Capital,* Volume I (London: Penguin Books, 1990 [1867]), pp. 169-172.

ACKNOWLEDGEMENTS

Versions of these essays first appeared in several publications and websites and I am grateful to their editors: *Black Renaissance Noire, Caribbean Beat, Caribbean Review of Books, Caribbean Literary Heritage, Electric Literature, Essay Daily, Prometheus Dreaming, Newsday, Jacket2, sxsalon, The Operating System, Wild Court, Zocalo Poets*, and *Seepersad and Sons: Naipaulian Synergies* (Leeds: Peepal Tree Press, 2019).

Thank you Jeremy Poynting, Sanjay Saith, Arnold Rampersad, Suzan Holder, Hannah Bannister, Robert Selby, Jess Zimmerman, Nicholas Laughlin, Kelly Baker Josephs, Quincy Troupe, Lynne DeSilva-Johnson, Alexander Best, J. Vijay Maharaj, Holly Bynoe, Rajiv Mohabir, Judy Raymond, Alison Donnell, Annalee Davis, Vahni Capildeo, Marina Salandy Brown, Claire Armitstead, Ann Marie Goodwin, Simone Hapel, Kenneth Ramchand, Christopher Cozier, Richard Rawlins, Sean Leonard, Loretta Collins Klobah, Monique Roffey, Opal Palmer Adisa, Mervyn Taylor, Breanne Mc Ivor, Caroline McKenzie, my family, and Chaplin, for his insightful analysis of the manuscript. All errors are mine.

INDEX

ABOUT THE AUTHOR

Andre Bagoo is a Trinidadian poet and writer. He is the author of *Trick Vessels* (Shearsman Books, 2012) and *BURN* (Shearsman Books, 2015) which was longlisted for the 2016 OCM Bocas Prize for Caribbean Literature, and *Pitch Lake* with Peepal Tree. His poetry has appeared at journals such as *Almost Island*, *Boston Review*, *Caribbean Review of Books*, *Draconian Switch*, *St Petersburg Review*, *The Poetry Review* and elsewhere. *The Undiscovered Country* is his fourth book.

ALSO BY ANDRE BAGOO

Pitch Lake
ISBN: 9781845233532; pp. 92; pub. 2017; £8.99

Divided into three sections , Andre Bagoo's poems explore the multiple resonances of the words, where pitch signifies both the stickiness of memory – the way the La Brea Pitch Lake is a place where "buried trees [are] born again" – and the idea of scattering: of places and impressions and the effort to hold them in one vision. The first part brings together poems that encompass reflections on art; Trinidad as a fallen Eden with its history of slavery and the inhumanity of "cachots brulants"; Black Lives Matter; visits to Britain and the image of cows "straight out of Hardy"; and poems about finding love in a climate of homophobia. Poems with an elaborate discursive structure sit next to little imagist poems written in response to Trinidad's disappearing fauna and threatened eco-system.

"Black Box" is a sequence of ekphrastic poems and responses to the work of writers as varied as Olive Senior, Langston Hughes and Walt Whitman.

"Lake", is a sequence of prose poems, varying in length, some surreal, suggestive rather than explicit, presenting subtly dislocated narratives that, even in a short space, disrupt the reader's expectations of where they are heading. In their brevity, these prose pieces offer surfaces, like that of a lake, that invite the reader to wonder what lies underneath but warn that this is not necessarily what is most predictable.

In *Pitch Lake*, Andre Bagoo, author of the Bocas prize shortlisted poetry collection, *BURN*, displays a continuing commitment to exploration and experiment.